PSION 5
in easy steps

Geoff Preston

COMPUTER
STEP

In easy steps is an imprint of Computer Step
Southfield Road . Southam
Warwickshire CV33 OFB . England

Tel: 01926 817999 Fax: 01926 817005
http://www.computerstep.com

Notice of Liability
Every effort has been made to ensure that this book contains accurate
and current information. However, Computer Step and the author shall
not be liable for any loss or damage suffered by readers as a result of
any information contained herein.

Trademarks
All trademarks are acknowledged as belonging to their respective
companies.

Printed and bound in the United Kingdom

ISBN 1-874029-87-3

Contents

8   In-built applications   77

9   Communications   139

10   Connecting a GPS receiver   153

Chapter One

Why use a Psion?

This chapter introduces the reasons for using a Psion Series 5 Computer and explains how it can help you manage your commitments.

Covers

Why use a Psion?

Many aspects of modern life require careful planning and organisation. It has been said that the tasks we have to perform can be divided into four types:

1. Urgent and important (meetings, crises, deadlines)

2. Urgent but not important (unsolicited interruptions, minor issues from others, mail, phone calls)

3. Not urgent but important (preparation, planning, relaxation)

4. Not urgent and not important either (trivia, irrelevant mail/phone calls, escape activities)

Many people find they are spending too much time on tasks in the first two categories in the mistaken belief that the urgent things must be done first. This is referred to as crisis management and is not an effective way of organising your life. Apart from all else, it is very stressful.

Most time-management tools concentrate on the urgent activities, yet research has shown that the most effective people concentrate their minds on the non-urgent but important issues such as careful planning and adequate preparation. This in turn enables people to deliver the tasks in the first two categories more effectively, leaving time to 'unwind' with some of the trivial tasks in the fourth category.

Your Psion Series 5 is currently the most powerful handheld computer available, by a wide margin. It is equipped with a variety of tools which will not only help you carry out many of the urgent tasks, but will also help you with the planning and preparation tasks. There are even programs on the Psion that help you to escape from it all.

What's the alternative?

A book-based personal diary or organiser is certainly an alternative, but only for some of the features you'll find in your Series 5. If you opt for a book-based organiser, you'll certainly have a good deal of change left over from what the Series 5 would have cost. But really all you'd be getting is an organiser and an address book, both of which are difficult to alter and – initially at least – can be time-consuming.

Entering the annual timetable of weekly meetings, for example, will require a new handwritten entry for every meeting. Using a Psion you can enter one, and reproduce it for the entire year, or even longer, making only 'custom' adjustments to some of the entries.

PSION SERIES 5 © Copyright Psion Computers PLC 1997
EPOC32 Platform © Copyright Psion Software PLC 1997
Version 1.00(113) - English (UK)
Worldwide patents pending

Writing an agenda for the Monday morning meeting would also be handwritten. That entry would then have to be edited, probably by rewriting, then typed by the secretary, checked by you and possibly amended again, before being printed, copied and then distributed.

A handwritten address book is fine, until someone moves. You then have to cross out the old address and enter the new one. Eventually you find you have not got enough space, so you have to enter it somewhere else – which means that it's no longer in alphabetical order, or that the entry is illegible.

Memos which are currently scribbled down on the back of an envelope and then lost can be typed into your Series 5 ready for printing, without the need to type it up at a later stage. If you carry a briefcase with you, then you've probably got room for a small printer which can print your letter whilst you are on the train or plane, ready to be posted when you arrive at your destination. Battery-powered printers mean that you're not confined to your desk to print, and you won't need to get yourself entangled with a lot of cables, since the transfer can be via infra-red signal.

Whilst you're sitting on the train, you could also sort out your finances or those of your company with the built-in spreadsheet.

If you use a mobile phone, you can send and receive faxes and email on the move. For the car traveller, your Series 5 can be used to help you plan your routes, and if you connect it to a global positioning system receiver you'll never get lost again.

Unlike a laptop computer which is actually very heavy to have on your lap for any length of time, the Series 5 palmtop computer can easily be used in your hand and quickly closed and slipped into your pocket. Wherever you currently use your book-based organiser, you could be using your Personal Digital Assistant, or PDA, as these products are generally known.

Over the coming months and years there will be a huge number of applications aimed at very specific markets. Language translators for travellers, prescription aids for doctors, flight planners for pilots and tidal data for sailors are some of the projected applications.

The Psion Series 5 computer is a diary, an organiser, a note taker, a letter writer, an address book, an alarm clock, a finance manager, a calculator, a sketch pad and much more besides. Learn to use as many of its features as possible. Some of the Series 5's features you may not know you need until you've learned how to use them, by which time you'll wonder how you managed before.

Chapter Two

Getting started

In this chapter, you'll learn about the general features of the Psion Series 5 computer, including information about batteries and general maintenance.

Covers

Batteries

After removing your computer from its box, the first job will be to insert the batteries. The Series 5 uses three batteries: a small lithium cell, which is supplied, and two AA batteries, which are not.

Backup battery

When the computer is new, the battery door may be quite stiff. To open the door, press it in slightly as you slide it out.

The lithium battery provides power to the computer when it's switched off. This is necessary to preserve both your work and the settings held in the computer, including the date and time. The battery is inserted behind a small door on the left of the computer.

The battery fits into the recess with the positive (+) side uppermost.

Main batteries

The computer will not run on the backup battery alone, as it cannot provide enough power. The main power comes from two AA-size batteries which are fitted behind a flap in the top edge of the computer. The batteries should be of the alkaline type and definitely not zinc carbon.

It is worth buying a multi-pack of good-quality batteries of a known brand. It is false economy to use cheap, unbranded batteries.

Rechargeable batteries can be used, but they are not ideal, as they go flat very quickly once they begin to lose their charge.

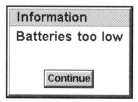

Towards the end of the batteries' life, some operations may not work, such as alarms, in which case a warning message will be displayed.

Switching on

When the computer is switched on for the first time, it will display the Psion Series 5 title screen. After that, the System screen is displayed. In future, when the computer is switched on, it will display the screen which was visible when the computer was last switched off.

The keyboard

HANDY TIP

Use a small battery-powered vacuum cleaner specially designed for keyboards to keep it clean.

The Psion 5's 54-key keyboard is probably the best small computer keyboard currently available. Apart from the usual letter, number and punctuation keys, there are a number of special keys which are used with other keys to access special characters or to perform particular functions.

The Shift keys will give capital letters if used with the letter keys, or will give the top characters on keys that have two characters on their face. (E.g. Shift+5 will give a % sign; Shift+full stop (.) will give a question mark (?).)

The Control key (Ctrl) is used with other keys to reproduce actions normally found in one of the menus.

The Function key (labelled Fn), which is situated on the bottom left of the keyboard between the Control (Ctrl) and Menu keys, will print the characters on the front edge of the keys. (E.g. Fn+4 will give '@'.)

Keyboard shortcuts

It's worth learning some of the keyboard shortcuts that are common to most programs. It is often quicker to use them than to use the wand.

Of all the keyboard shortcuts, the following are some of the most useful and apply to all programs.

Ctrl+E	Exit a program (also saves current work)
Ctrl+N	Create a new file
Ctrl+P	Print current file
Ctrl+A	Select or mark all
Ctrl+X	Cut marked text or graphic (delete and place in clipboard)
Ctrl+C	Copy marked text or graphic into clipboard
Ctrl+V	Paste text or graphic from clipboard
Ctrl+Z	Undo

You will probably find that some of the tasks you frequently carry out with the Series 5 will have their own shortcut. Thoughtfully, the programmers have included the keyboard shortcuts on the menus, which makes them easier to remember.

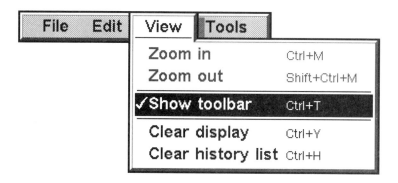

The screen

Use only the special wand to touch the screen, as anything else could damage it.

The Psion Series 5's screen is one of the largest available on a palmtop computer and is touch-sensitive. A special touch wand is used to touch icons (small pictures) on the screen to make selections and to operate the programs. In fact, apart from entering textual information, almost all of the functions of the computer and its in-built applications can be controlled by touching the screen. The touch wand is stored on the right-hand side of the case, towards the back. Press it in and release and it will pop out of its housing.

You should never use an ink pen, as you could get ink on the screen, which may be difficult or impossible to remove. You also should not use your finger to touch the screen for three reasons. Firstly, your finger is too large and will not be accurate enough; secondly, you could scratch the screen; and thirdly, using your finger makes the screen very messy!

Screen contrast

The screen's contrast may be adjusted in two ways. The first method is via the Control Panel in the System screen. After opening the Control Panel, touch the screen icon and a dialog will open. You may enter the contrast setting in the strip.

Because of the nature of the screen, there is a certain amount of reflection. Try to position the computer to minimise this.

Alternatively, Fn+M or Fn+? will alter the contrast.

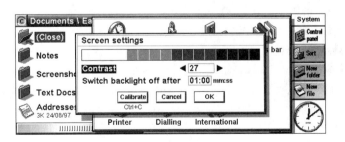

Calibrating the screen

If you feel that the computer is consistently failing to exactly pinpoint the spot where you touch the screen, it may be that the screen needs recalibrating. Although this sounds serious, there is a simple program to help you do this.

From the System screen, touch the Control Panel button and then touch the Screen icon. Next touch the Calibrate button to run the calibration program.

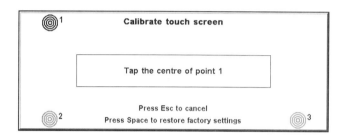

You will be asked to touch a dot at the centre of three circles. Locate the dots very carefully and touch them as accurately as possible. If you think you've done a good job, touch the Accept New Settings button.

Cleaning the screen

Opinion is divided about the best method of cleaning the screen. Personally I find that tissue such as toilet tissue or disposable hankies create paper dust which will fall into the keyboard.

REMEMBER

Always switch off before cleaning the screen.

I find that a soft cloth designed for cleaning spectacles is much better, and if really necessary, your optician can supply a mild spray cleaner which should be used sparingly. It should be sprayed on the cloth, not on the screen.

Keep the cloth in its protective case, and only use it for your Series 5.

Dialogs, menus and toolbars

In this chapter, you'll learn about the ways in which you can interact with your Psion Series 5 Computer via the on-screen dialogs, menus and toolbars.

Chapter Three

Covers

Overview

Around the screen are a number of bars containing icons which operate special functions or start programs. Two of them are permanent and provide general shortcuts, whilst the others can be displayed and removed as required. These contain shortcuts which are specific to the active program.

At the bottom of the screen is a permanent icon bar. When one of the program icons is touched, you will be taken directly to that program or the last file used with that program.

The icon on the left (System) will always take you back to the System screen.

The icon on the right (Extras) will place an on-screen icon bar at the bottom of the screen, on which will be the icons for some additional programs. Touching on one of these icons will enter that program.

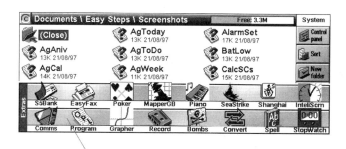

This is the Extras bar showing the additional programs available. *Initially* there will be five extra programs.

Permanent toolbars

The Menu icon on the toolbar is exactly equivalent to the Menu key on the keyboard.

The toolbar on the left of the screen contains buttons for shortcuts to four commonly used functions which are appropriate to most programs.

Under the menu icon is the editing suite, which leads to a menu with three options: Cut, Copy and Paste. These are only of use in programs which will allow these functions to take place (e.g., if you try to open this menu while playing the Bombs game, a message will tell you that this function is not available).

At the bottom of the left-hand toolbar are the magnifying symbols, which you can use to zoom up or down. Clicking on these has just the same effect as using the keyboard shortcuts Ctrl+M (zoom in) and Shift+Ctrl+M (zoom out).

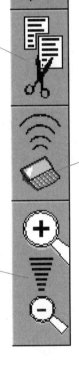

Touching the top icon will display the menu bar appropriate for the current screen (i.e., the menu bar displayed in the System screen will be different from that shown in the Calculator program).

Immediately under the editing icon is the infra-red transmit and receive icon. Touching this leads to a menu asking whether you intend to transmit or receive infra-red data. Once again, this is only relevant for programs where transmission of data is possible.

On-screen toolbars

Apart from closing open files, the Open files/programs dialog is a quick way of moving between programs, and is especially helpful if you're moving data between applications.

On the right is an on-screen toolbar which can be added and removed either from the menu structure or by pressing Ctrl+T. The contents of this toolbar will depend on which program is running. There is usually a block of four buttons which contain functions specific to the particular program.

The panel at the top of the toolbar will contain either the name of the program or the name of the current file, or 'System' if in the System screen. Touching it will lead to a dialog box listing all currently open files.

When the *Open files/programs* dialog opens, the name of the file from which it was opened will be highlighted. Touching the name of one of the other files will highlight that one. From there you may either close it, go to it (possibly to continue work on it) or escape from the dialog by pressing Escape or touching Done.

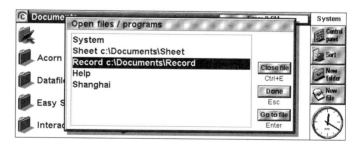

The clock will normally be displayed at the bottom of the toolbar. Touching it will change it from analogue to digital format.

Dialogs

A dialog is a window into which you may enter a choice or selection. Dialogs contain legends, with text-entry boxes alongside. When you click on a text-entry box, an arrow will appear at each end.

1 Touch the arrows to scroll through the available choices. This may be quite a long list of choices, or the choice of a tick or no tick.

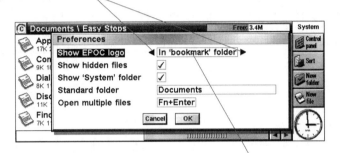

2 Touching the panel a second time will either display the available choices as a menu or place the cursor in the text-entry box for you to type in the relevant information. Touching one of the items from the list will place it into the text-entry box.

3 To abort the selection, touch Cancel or press Escape. To confirm the selection, touch OK or press Enter.

Calendar

In a dialog where a date is required, touching the text-entry box twice will display a calendar with today's date circled.

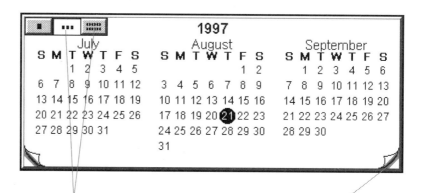

Initially, the calendar for the current month only is shown, but touching one of the three buttons at the top left of the calendar will change the display to either three months or a whole year.

Each calendar has a 'turned up page' at the bottom left and right to enable you to turn to the next or previous page.

Scroll bars

When there is more data than can be displayed on the screen or in a window on the screen, a vertical and/or horizontal scroll bar appears to allow you to scroll the screen up, down or across to view more data.

1 Touch and drag the slider itself up, down or sideways to scroll quickly.

2 Touch the up and down arrows or the left and right buttons to scroll slowly. Each touch will nudge the window up, down or sideways by one line.

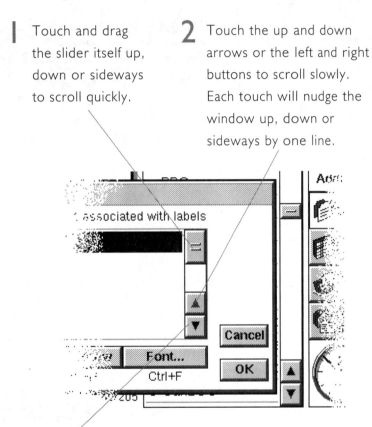

3 To scroll the window smoothly, hold the wand down on one of the arrows.

4 Touch the wand either side of the slider to move up or down by one full screen.

Selecting from menus

All of the options and functions for all programs can be accessed from the menus. In addition, some commonly used options may be found as keyboard shortcuts, on 'buttons' on the screen, or on one of the toolbars.

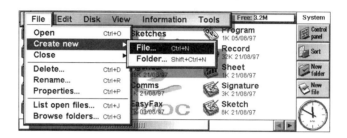

The menu structure is accessed by either pressing the Menu key or touching the icon at the very top of the left-hand toolbar.

Select one of the menu headings to display the list of options associated with that category.

The menu system comprises a menu bar at the top of the screen, on which are a number of words which may be regarded as categories.

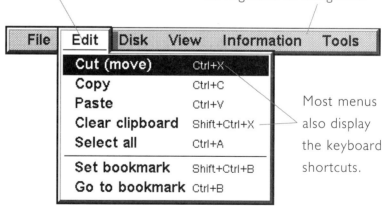

Most menus also display the keyboard shortcuts.

Another word on the menu bar may be selected by either touching it with the wand or moving one of the left or right arrow keys at the bottom right of the keyboard.

Once the correct menu has been located, touching the wand on the required option (or moving the up or down arrow keys on the bottom right of the keyboard and pressing Enter) will select that option.

On some menus, items have arrows alongside them, and these lead to other sub-menus which may be navigated through either by touching the arrow with the wand, using the right arrow key or pressing Enter.

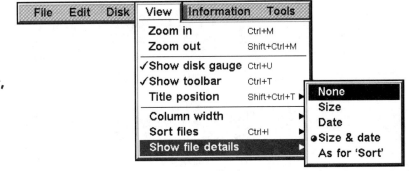

Remember, the menu structure differs for each program.

Menus may be cancelled by either touching the menu icon on the top left of the screen again, or by pressing the Menu or Escape keys.

On-screen help

If you are stuck on a particular point, the Psion Series 5 has a built-in help facility containing 271 useful hints and tips, which may be able to provide the answer you are looking for.

To begin the Help application, press Fn+/ (the key immediately to the right of the spacebar).

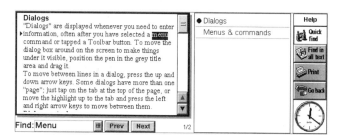

There are two ways to search for help for a particular topic. The first is to browse through the topics on the right of the screen.

Use the scroll bar to move through the list of help topics.

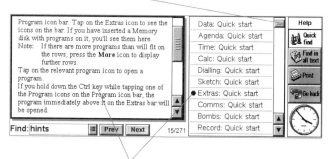

2 When you see a heading that looks helpful, touch it with the wand. The full help text will appear in the left-hand box.

The second, and usually the quickest method, is to get the computer to search for the topic you require.

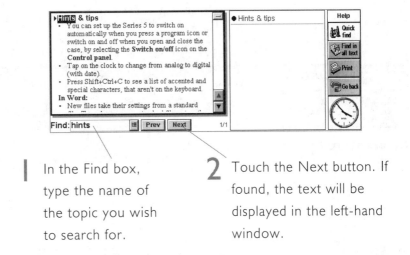

1 In the Find box, type the name of the topic you wish to search for.

2 Touch the Next button. If found, the text will be displayed in the left-hand window.

Text which appears in the left-hand window can be marked, copied and pasted into another document.

1 Mark a piece of text by dragging the wand over it so that it is inverted (white becomes black and black becomes white).

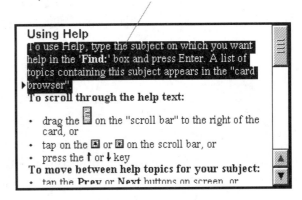

2 Open the Edit menu (second button on the left-hand toolbar) and touch Copy.

...contd

3 Open the document into which you wish to paste the text and touch the wand at the place where you wish the text to be inserted.

4 Open the Edit menu again and touch Paste. The text will be inserted into the document at the current cursor position.

You can print the current help card by pressing Ctrl+P.

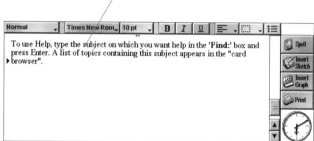

When a new application is installed into your Series 5, it may have a help file supplied with it.

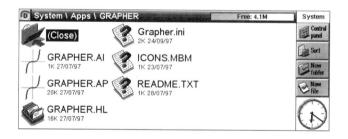

It's always worth looking at and can usually be accessed from within the program by opening the menu bar and selecting Information>Help.

Once in Help, touching the Go Back button on the right-hand toolbar will return you to the application you were previously using.

When you've finished with Help, close it down to conserve memory.

Chapter Four

Personalising the settings

In this chapter, you'll learn how to set up your Psion
Series 5 ready for use in the way in which you prefer to
use it, by altering the settings from the Control Panel.

Covers

Personalising your Series 5

Once the batteries have been installed and the Psion has been switched on, you will be presented with the System screen.

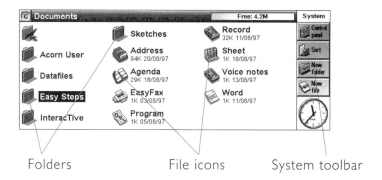

Folders   File icons   System toolbar

On the main part of the screen will be the files available with their icons, and on the right the System toolbar. Touching the Control Panel icon will display a window containing 10 icons.

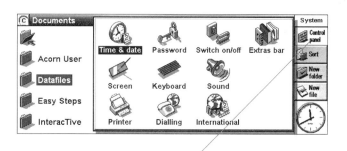

Touch the Control Panel button to open the
Control Panel, touch it again to close it.

You won't need to alter all of them now, but it's certainly worth spending some time on this as it will make your computer easier to use for your specific needs or likes, and it is an excellent way to start using your computer and to practise using the touch wand.

Touch the close button to return to the Control Panel.

🕿 Time and date

A particularly useful feature is the in-built clock and calendar, which can display the time and date on every screen if desired. Touch the wand onto the Time & date icon twice and another window showing a large analogue clock will appear. Touch the top button (Time & date) and a dialog will be displayed into which you enter the current time (initially use 12-hour format, although this can be changed to 24-hour format).

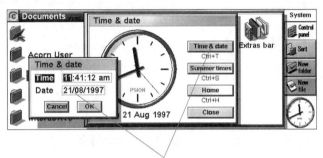

The Psion's internal clock is very accurate, so it is worth getting the exact time from either the speaking clock (dial 123) or teletext.

Touching each button opens a dialog in which you can enter time-related details.

Enter the time slightly ahead of what it actually is, say 11:53:00 am when the time is actually 11:51:31 am. That will give you enough time to set the date and then watch for the actual time to come round to the time you've entered in your Series 5.

As soon as the times match, touch the OK button to set the time. Next, set the summer times and the home city. When touching the various fields on each box, arrowheads will appear on each side of the field. Touching these will scroll through the possible choices. For tick boxes, touching the box will switch the tick on or off.

Password and owner info

If you intend to hold information in your Psion that you don't want others to see, then it should be password-protected. Double-touching the Password icon in the Control Panel for the first time leads to a dialog where you can enter personal details (name, address, telephone number etc.), determine when the personal information will be displayed, and enter a password.

Not all insurance companies auto-matically insure portable computer equipment. Make sure it is insured for its full value, especially when it is taken out of your home.

| Touch the Owner info button and enter as much contact information as you feel comfortable with. Remember, like all portable items, there is a chance that you may leave it somewhere. If someone picks it up and switches it on, the first thing they'll see is who it belongs to and who to contact to return it. On the subject of losing your Psion, you should check your household insurance.

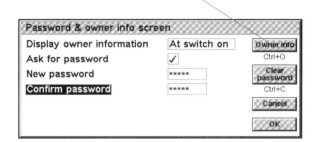

The Psion password system is very, very secure. If you forget your password, there is no way you'll ever get into your Series 5 other than resetting it, in which case you'll lose all of your work and all of the settings.

2 Choose a password and enter it into the New Password box. The password should be something which is easy to remember and not too long: 5–8 characters is usually fine. Unlike the Series 3/3a/3c, the password is case-sensitive and so 'Sunny' and 'sunny' would be regarded as different.

3 You will also need to confirm your password by re-entering it. The reason for entering the password twice is to ensure you haven't mis-typed the word.

Unique ID

Each Psion Series 5 computer has its own unique identification number, which may be found by entering the menus from the System screen and going to Information> Machine. Make a note of this number and keep it safe. If you should 'lose' your Series 5, your insurance company and possibly the police might want to know what it is. You should also pass the number to the Stolen Psion Registry. The address is in the last chapter.

 Record the ID number in the document-ation about your Series 5 and in your home inventory.

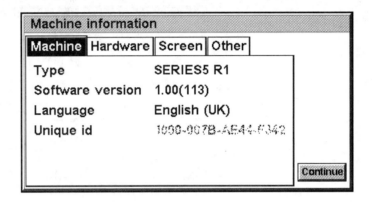

You can enter your unique ID below:

....

Switching on and off

The Psion computer is very efficient in respect of its power consumption. However, like all battery-powered items, the frequency with which the batteries need replacing is largely determined by the way it is used. The Switch on/off dialog lets you set the computer to switch off automatically. Doing so will significantly improve battery life.

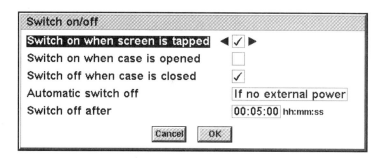

You have several choices, including switching off when the case is closed, but initially set it so that it will switch itself off after 3 minutes of inactivity (i.e., no keys pressed and the screen not touched). If you have a power pack whereby the computer can be run from the mains rather than batteries, it's a good idea to set the 'Automatic switch off' option to 'If no external power'.

Just as there are switch-off options, so there are switch-on options. Apart from using the On key (the same key as Escape), you can choose to have the computer switch itself on when the case is opened, and/or when the screen is tapped with the wand. A good initial configuration is to have it switch on when the screen is touched and switch off when case is closed, or after 3:00 minutes of inactivity if there is no external power.

Screen

The two functions performed from this dialog are screen contrast and backlight duration. The screen contrast should be adjusted to suit personal taste and may depend on the lighting conditions at the time. The contrast adjustment can also be carried out using Fn+M (lighter) and Fn+? (darker); this may be considered a more convenient method.

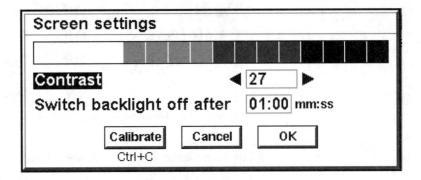

One special feature of the Series 5 is its backlit screen, which enables it to be used in poor lighting conditions. As effective as it is, it consumes a large amount of power from the batteries. The backlight (which can be switched on and off with Fn+spacebar) should be set to automatically switch off after 30 seconds to 1 minute of inactivity.

In use, there is a slight humming sound when the backlight is on. This is quite normal.

 # Sound

The volume of three sounds can be controlled from this dialog. Some people will prefer to have their computer set to be as quiet as possible, but this is not always a good idea.

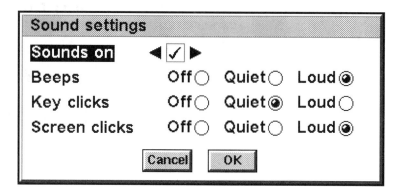

It's debatable whether there's much point in the computer clicking each time a key is pressed, but it is worth having an audible click when the screen is touched to confirm that what you've asked for has been accepted.

 # Printer

The computer needs to know what printer is connected, and this requires the correct printer driver to be selected. There are initially six printer-specific drivers pre-programmed into the Series 5, and in due course others will be available on disk which can be installed into the Series 5.

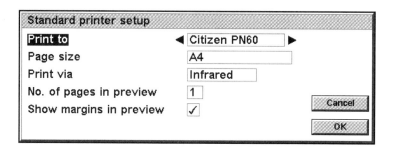

The printer drivers pre-programmed into the Series 5 are:

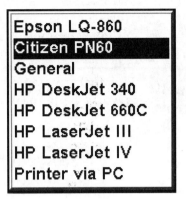

There is also a General printer driver, which will print out text only to most printers. It will not output any layout or any highlights such as italics or bold.

It is also possible to print via your PC.

The page size will normally be A4, although there is the opportunity to use other sizes, including envelopes.

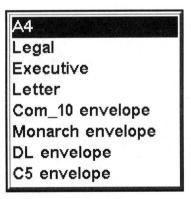

If using a parallel printer, you must select parallel in the next field. The other settings can be left for the time being.

# Dialling

Modern telephones use tones, DTMF tones to be precise. Sending these tones down the phone line calls the number, and normally the buttons on the phone do this for you. However, the Psion Series 5 can also send the tones so that a phone number in a data file, for instance, can actually be used to dial the number for you.

This feature may not work well with some portable phones.

BEWARE

This feature may seem a little gimmicky at first, but it really is worth being patient and getting it working.

Settings for dialling phone numbers

Dial out code	9
Tone time	6 1/32 sec
Delay time	4 1/32 sec
Pause time	32 1/32 sec

Type in the box to test dialling

9,123

Country	Test dial	Cancel	OK
Tab	Space		

If you intend using this feature from home, all you need do is remove the dial out code. If you intend using this from your workplace where your phone goes through an internal switchboard, you need to insert the number needed to obtain an outside line. Normally this will be 9.

To use the automatic dialling, pick up the telephone receiver, hold the Series 5 about 6 inches away from the handset and press the space bar. You should get the speaking clock. If it doesn't work first time, make sure you have a dialling tone and try altering the interval between tones.

International settings

Opening the International settings reveals a tabbed dialog box. Each tab is a separate dialog, and when the tab is touched it will bring the relevant dialog to the front. The tabs are for Time, Date, Number, Currency and Units.

Time. The most likely change you'll want to make is to decide whether to use 24-hour or 12-hour time, and whether the clock is an analogue or digital one.

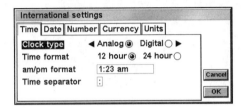

Date. You may set the format for the date, the start of the week and the days in your working week. This information is used by Agenda and by the alarms in the Time application.

Number. This is to do with the way numbers are displayed. You have the choice of using a full stop or a comma to represent decimals, and whether you wish thousands to be separated with a comma.

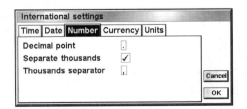

Currency. You may declare the symbol you require to represent the currency you're most likely to use, and the preferred currency format.

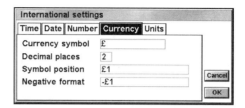

Units. This is your opportunity to declare whether you wish to use imperial or metric units for short and long distances and other measurements.

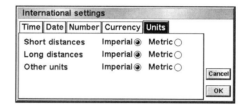

Keyboard

This dialog will set the rate at which the keys will automatically repeat. When a key is pressed, the character is printed on the screen. If the key is held, it will begin to repeat. The first entry in this dialog determines the time between the first character being printed and the second one. You may enter a number between 200 and 2000.

HANDY TIP

It's probably not necessary to alter the keyboard until after you have used the Series 5 for a while.

After the first repeat, you may enter the time for subsequent repeats. Any number between 20 and 2000 may be entered.

New documents

In this chapter, you'll learn how to start and exit programs, and how to create and save new documents on your Psion Series 5.

Chapter Five

Covers

Starting a program

There are three ways to start a program or open a document on the Series 5.

1   The first method is to double-touch the required document icon on the System screen. This will open the file and display it exactly as it was left, including the position of the cursor.

2   The second method is to touch one of the icons on the icon bar at the bottom of the screen. Regardless of what you are currently doing, that program will be started and it will usually open the last file it had seen. If the last file seen has been moved or renamed, it will open a blank document.

3   The third method is in fact a variation of the first method and involves using the arrow keys to move the highlight bar to the icon of your choice and then pressing Enter.

Exiting a program

Like all Psion palmtops, the Series 5 is a true multitasking computer. This means that several programs can be run at the same time and that data can be passed between the documents in the various programs.

However, when a document is not being used it should be closed down so as to conserve memory and processor time.

Closing files can be done in several ways. From outside the program you wish to close (i.e., from the System screen or from within another program), if the right-hand toolbar is visible, touch the top box (System).

This will open a dialog listing all open documents. Touch the one you wish to close and then touch Close File to close it, then Done to remove the dialog.

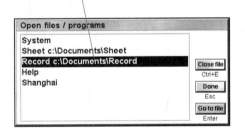

To close the current document from within the document itself, touch the top icon on the right-hand toolbar to open the dialog. The name of the document will be highlighted. Touch Close file and then Done. This can also be achieved from the menu bar by selecting File>Close, or by pressing Ctrl+E.

Alternatively, from the System screen, highlight the document to be closed and press Ctrl+E, or press Shift+Ctrl+E to save and close down all open documents.

Creating new documents

There are two ways to create a new document. Each method has a small but significant difference.

If you find that a program has stopped working and that you cannot exit from it using any of the usual methods (Ctrl+E from within the program, Ctrl+E from the System screen or from the Open files> Programs dialogue), try Shift+Ctrl+Fn+K from within the program.

1 Whilst in the System screen, touch the New File button, or from the menu bar select File>Create New>File, or use the keyboard shortcut Ctrl+N.

2 The dialog below appears. Enter a file name and a program type. This will create a file with the standard settings.

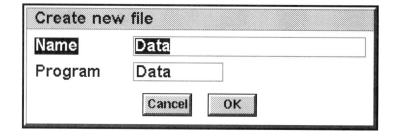

The other method is to create a new file from within another file.

When you create a new file or a new folder, it will normally be placed in the System screen currently displayed.

Open a file and then create a new document by either pressing Ctrl+N or by selecting Create new file from the menu bar. In this case, the new document will have the same setup characteristics as the file from which it was created. For example, a data file created in this way would have the same labels or fields as the previous file, whereas a file created from the System screen would contain the default labels.

If you wish to open more than one document belonging to the same program, hold down the Fn key when opening the second document.

With two documents from the same program opened, touching the program icon on the icon bar at the bottom of the screen will switch between the two.

If three or more documents are open, touching the program icon will go through the documents in the order in which they were opened.

Saving documents

Exiting a program automatically saves the document. You can force the program to save the document without exiting the program by pressing Ctrl+S. When a document is saved, it overwrites the previous version, and consequently the earlier version will be lost.

In most cases this is exactly what you want to happen, but sometimes you may not want the old version to be destoyed.

If you have opened a file and made some alterations to it, but you are unhappy about the alterations you made, press Ctrl+R to revert to the old version.

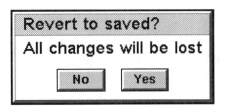

You'll be asked if you really wish to do this, because the version you are using will be lost unless it has been saved elsewhere.

...contd

You may prevent the loss of old files in two ways: either change the name of the file or change its stored location.

Press Shift+Ctrl+S to open the Save As dialog, which contains three text-entry boxes. You may enter information into any or all of these, but to preserve your old file you must alter at least one.

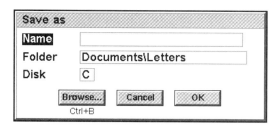

All future attempts to save will place the document in the last location chosen and with the last file name used.

The top panel will be blank. Leaving it blank will use the original file name when the document is next saved. Entering a different file name will force all future save operations to use the new name, and the file will be placed alongside the older version.

The middle text-entry box contains the location of the old file. You may choose another location by double-touching the text box. Finally, you may choose a different disk by selecting the appropriate letter from the third text box.

Memory management

In this chapter, you'll learn about the ways in which you can keep the files on your Psion Series 5 tidy and ordered.

Chapter Six

Overview

The Series 5 has a great deal of memory and is therefore capable of holding a large number of files. It is most important that you organise your files very carefully.

Just as you might store various papers in cardboard wallets, so you should store the files you created on your Series 5 in folders.

The names of the folders should relate to what they are going to contain (e.g. Letters, Bank Account, Homework etc.).

Creating a new folder

| Go to the System screen and either select File>Create new>Folder, or press Shift+Ctrl+N. The following dialog will open for you to enter the name of the new folder.

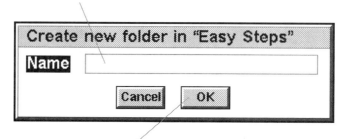

When you create a new file or a new folder, it will be placed in the system screen currently displayed.

2 Click OK when you have entered a name.

Although you can use a folder name up to 250+ characters long, about 20 characters is usually more than enough to adequately describe the contents. When choosing a name, you may use any keyboard character, including numbers, except for the following characters:

/   <   >   :   \   ?

...contd

You might begin by creating a folder called Work, and placing other folders within that. It will keep the disk space tidy and will also make backing up your work a great deal simpler.

You may create folders within folders, enabling you to subdivide work. For example, you might have a folder called Letters, and inside that you might have a folder called Sales, another called Memos, another called Personal, etc. Those folders can also have folders inside them.

Creating a new file

1 Creating files is similar to creating folders. Either touch the New File button or press Ctrl+N in the System screen to open the Create New File dialog.

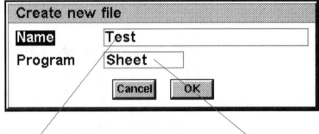

It really is important to begin storing your files in a methodical way. It can be a laborious task to try and rectify it later.

2 In the top strip, enter the name of the file you wish to create.

3 In the lower strip, choose the program you wish to use to create the new file.

4 Touch OK or press Enter to confirm.

Backing up files

HANDY TIP

Remember, the longer you leave between backups, the more work could be irretrievably lost. Try to make backups each day.

The fact that your Psion Series 5 is portable means that there is a greater chance of you losing it. Although the computer itself may be insured against loss or theft, the work painstakingly created and stored in the computer will not be. Therefore, it is even more important that you keep copies of your files and keep them up to date. In other words, take backups regularly.

You can back up the contents of your Series 5 in three ways:

- on to a PC using PsiWin 2
- on to a Series 5 CompactFlash memory card
- on to a dedicated floppy disk drive

If you have a PC, then by far the cheapest way to back up your files is by using PsiWin 2, which was supplied with your Series 5.

Installing PsiWin2

PsiWin2 should be installed on your PC's hard disk.

In the System screen of your Series 5, enter Ctrl+L to open the remote link setup dialog.

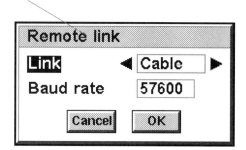

2 Initially, set the link to Cable...

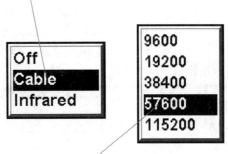

3 ...and the fastest speed your PC will accept. This is likely to be at least 38400, but if you have a faster serial port, choose that. The Series 5 can be set as high as 115200.

4 Press Enter or touch OK to confirm your choices.

5 Connect the docking lead supplied to the Series 5 (the port is at the back on the left) and connect the other end to the serial port of your PC.

6 Insert the PsiWin2 CD-ROM into the CD drive on your PC, double-click on My Computer and then on the CD-ROM drive icon containing the PsiWin2 CD-ROM.

...contd

7 Double-click on Setup to install PsiWin2 on your PC. The installation program will guide you through the installation of the software on your PC and will also place a couple of files in the system folder of your Series 5.

The serial link must be on. To switch it on, go to the System screen, press Ctrl+L, then choose Cable and the fastest speed your PC can use.

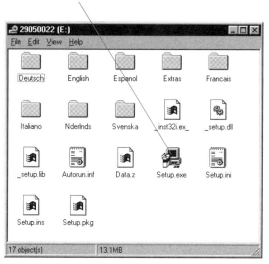

Using PsiWin2

Having installed PsiWin on your PC, it's a simple job to make a complete backup of the Series 5.

| Simply click the right-hand button on the My Psion icon and select Backup.

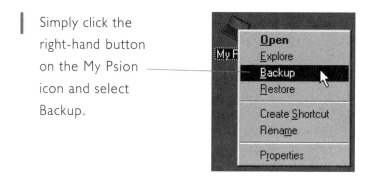

2 Alternatively, double-clicking with the left-hand mouse button on the My Psion icon will open a window which can be used to copy individual files or groups of files between the Series 5 and the PC.

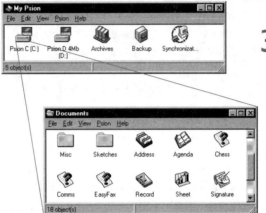

3 After opening *My Psion*, double-click on the left icon to display the contents of the Series 5's main memory.

4 To copy a single file between the Series 5 and the PC (or the other way), drag the file from one window to another by placing the mouse pointer over the file to be copied, holding down the left mouse button and dragging into the destination window.

5 If you drag with the right-hand mouse button, a menu will open offering the choice of copying or moving. You may also elect to have the computer convert the file from native Psion format to a PC-compatible format.

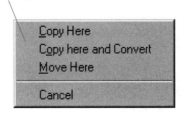

Memory cards

As there is only space for one memory card, it makes sense to buy the largest possible (or affordable).

Former users of Series 3, 3a and 3c computers will be pleased to learn that the Solid State Disks (SSDs) that were so expensive have been replaced with much cheaper industry-standard CompactFlash memory cards in either 2 Mb, 4 Mb or 10 Mb sizes. Larger sizes, possibly as large as 100 Mb, will become available in due course.

Although they are memory devices, they are often referred to as disks, as they are used in the same way as a disk drive in a larger computer. Memory disks are inserted behind the door on the right-hand edge of the computer and can be used like a second disk drive to load files to be worked on.

In keeping with PC conventions, the second disk is referred to as Drive D (the main disk is C).

It is possible to use the CompactFlash card from a digital camera, although it will need to be formatted on the Series 5, which will erase all data previously held on the card. As some digital cameras do not have formatting facilities built in, a CompactFlash card might not, therefore, be able to be used in a camera after it had been used with the Series 5. However, they are much cheaper than the official Psion CompactFlash and are currently available in 2 Mb, 4 Mb, 8 Mb, 16 Mb and 32 Mb versions.

Some Compact Flash cards require 5 volts to operate. These will not work in the Series 5, which requires 3.5 volt devices.

If using CompactFlash cards from a digital camera you will almost always have to format them. However, even if you don't have to, it's worth doing anyway, as it might provide you with a slightly larger disk. (An 8 Mb CompactFlash card will normally give 7.7 or 7.8 Mb when formatted.)

Formatting a CompactFlash card

When CompactFlash cards are purchased, they are usually ready to use. Normally they will be blank, although they may sometimes have some files or utilities on them. These can be deleted in the normal way (touch and then press Delete) or by formatting.

Formatting is a process which 'sets up' the CompactFlash card ready for use.

Be absolutely sure you are formatting the correct disk. Formatting removes all data from the disk, and it can never be recovered.

1 From the System screen, open the menu bar and choose Disk>Format disk.

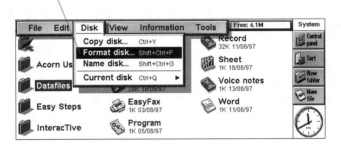

2 A dialog will open into which you must enter the name of the drive. You may also select a name for the disk at the same time. (To avoid confusion, name your Psion disks something different to your PC disks. Calling the main drives on both computers 'Drive C' is not wise.)

Unlike the SSDs used in the Series 3a and 3c, CompactFlash recovers its memory when items are erased. (The only way to recover memory from Flash SSDs is to format them.)

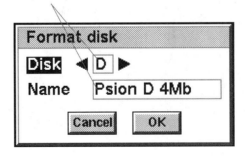

3 Touch OK or press Enter to begin formatting.

A dedicated disk drive

At least two companies are currently working on a large storage device for the Series 5. This could be based on a 3.5" floppy disk drive, or a much larger device which can be linked directly to the Series 5 so that files and software can be backed up on to a floppy disk or other magnetic media. The drives can be either mains- or battery-powered. Even if you've got a PC, this is still worth considering, as it will enable you to make back ups 'on the move'. The cost of the drive is only slightly more than that of a mid-size CompactFlash card, but the cost of the disks is negligible.

Once the software for connecting such a drive to a Series 5 is finished, you'll have a very cheap, high-capacity storage device which will also enable you to transfer files between the Series 5 and a PC without the need for using PsiWin2.

Moving, copying and deleting files

As the Series 5 only displays the contents of one folder at a time, dragging files from one folder and dropping them into another clearly isn't possible. But Psion have made moving files around just as simple by allowing you to use the Edit menu (Cut, Copy and Paste), which is the second icon on the left-hand toolbar.

HANDY TIP

If a file of the same name exists in the destination screen, you'll be asked to confirm that you do want to continue. If you do, the file being copied will overwrite and consequently destroy the other file.

Moving files

1 To move a single file, locate it and touch it once.

2 Open the Edit menu and select Cut. You'll notice the file icon inherits a dotted frame around it.

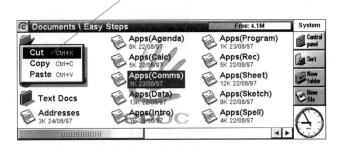

3 Open the folder you wish to move the file into, open the Edit menu again and select Paste. The file will be moved (i.e. deleted from its original home and copied into the new location).

HANDY TIP

This method works not only for files, but also for folders.

4 If, after touching a file and selecting Cut from the menu, you change your mind, reselect Cut and the dotted marker around the file icon will be removed.

Copying files

Copying is the same, except that you choose Copy rather than Cut from the Edit menu. Copying a file will leave the original file in its place and add a duplicate in the selected destination.

...contd

Multiple files and/or folders may also be copied. There are two ways of making multiple selections, both of which mimic the method used in Microsoft Windows. The first method is to touch one file or folder to select it and then, whilst holding down the Shift key, touch a second file or folder. All the files and folders between the two will have been selected. You may then proceed by opening the Edit menu and either cutting or copying, followed by pasting.

The second method requires the use of the Control (Ctrl) key. Again, select the first file as before, then whilst holding Ctrl, touch any other folders or files you wish and they too will be selected. The problem with this method is that if you're left-handed you have to either hold the wand in your right hand, or use your right hand on the only Ctrl key, which is on the left of the keyboard.

Deleting files
To delete a file or a folder, simply select it (or more than one using one of the methods previously described) and press Delete. You will be asked to confirm that this is what you want to do, and in the case of a folder, if you wish to delete all of the contents.

 In this case, pressing Enter will not have the same effect as touching the Yes button.

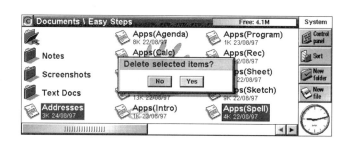

File protection

To protect your files against accidental erasure, you may lock them or hide them.

 Don't forget to go back to Tools> Preferences and deselect 'Show hidden files' so that the other files you want to be hidden, will be.

1 To protect a file or files, go to the System screen, select the file or files you wish to protect, open the menu bar and go to File>Properties.

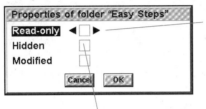

2 If you choose Read only, then you will not be able to make any changes to the file, including deleting it.

3 For further protection, you can hide a file, in which case it will not even appear on the System screen. Select Hidden from the Properties dialog.

4 To unlock a file, return to the Properties dialog and deselect Read-only.

Making a hidden file visible again is a little trickier, as it's not able to be selected (because it can't be seen!).

1 In the System screen menu, go to Tools>Preferences and choose Show hidden files. This will reveal all hidden files.

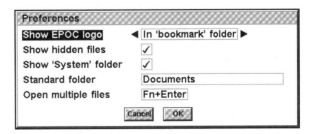

2 Select the file you wish to 'unhide', then return to File>Properties and deselect Hidden.

The bookmark

In a System screen, pressing Shift+Ctrl+B will set that screen as the bookmarked screen.

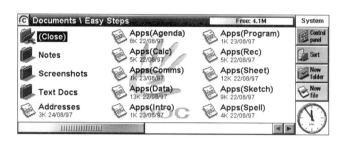

If you open the menus in the System screen and go to Tools>Preferences, you can choose to have the EPOC logo displayed only on the bookmarked screen.

Wherever you wander in the system screens, Ctrl+B will always take you straight back to the bookmarked screen, regardless of which disk you are currently viewing.

If, however, you choose to set the bookmark on a removable disk, and that disk is subsequently removed and replaced with another, the bookmarked screen will be lost until either another screen is chosen as the bookmark or the card containing the bookmark is replaced.

The Disk Information bar

You can check on the remaining disk space using the Disk Information bar, which can be displayed either on the left or at the top of the screen.

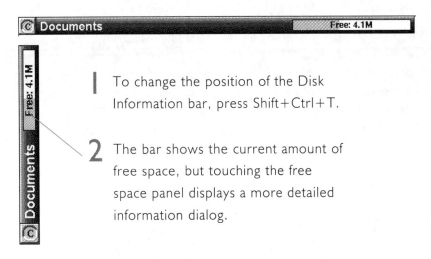

1 To change the position of the Disk Information bar, press Shift+Ctrl+T.

2 The bar shows the current amount of free space, but touching the free space panel displays a more detailed information dialog.

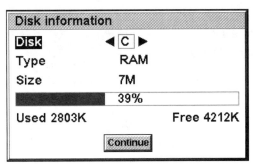

Browsing

Whilst the Series 5 has its own filing system, it is not dissimilar to the PC's filing system. Files (programs and documents) are stored within folders. Folders may contain files or other folders. This means that although versatile, work can get buried within deep folder structures, which can make it a little difficult to find using the usual method of double-touching the Close folder icon and then double-touching on a folder to open it.

...contd

You may not open a file or start a program from the browser, but merely locate it.

Touching the Disk Information bar at the top or left side of the screen will open the browser with the currently selected files visible. In other words, if the System screen looks like this...

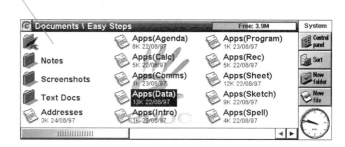

...then the browser will look like this.

You can use the cursor (arrow) keys to move the highlight up and down.

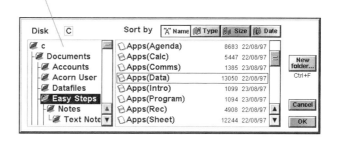

Touching a folder on the left of the screen will open the folder and reveal the contents in the right-hand part of the screen.

When the browser is closed, it returns to the System screen with the same folder or file highlighted. Therefore, if the browser looks like this...

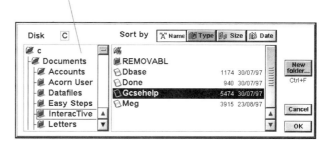

....the System screen will look like this.

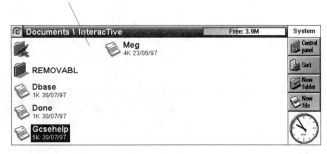

This will enable you to easily locate and mark a file, so that when you return to the System screen you'll be able to start it immediately.

At the top left of the browser screen is a disk-selection dialog. Touch the box to reveal the arrows, which will skip between the currently available disks.

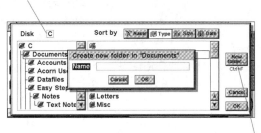

Once you have located the area of the computer's memory you require, you can create a new folder by touching the New Folder button to display a standard Create Folder dialog.

Files displayed in the browser may be sorted by either...

> **Name** – in alphabetical order
>
> **Type** – folders first
>
> **Size** of the file
>
> **Date** when last modified

...by touching the appropriate button at the top right of the screen.

File details

You may choose to have additional file information displayed in the System screens along with the file name.

Select View>Show File Details, and a menu containing four options will be displayed.

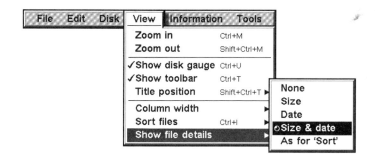

You may choose to display either no additional information, the size of the file, the date the file was created or last altered, the size and the date, or the last option, *As for 'Sort'*.

If you choose *As for 'Sort'*, the additional information displayed with the file names will be relevant to the order in which you have chosen to sort the files on screen. For example, if the files are sorted by date, then only the date will be displayed along with the file name.

Printing documents

In this chapter, you'll learn how to connect a printer to your Psion Series 5 and print files. The chapter also examines the ways in which you can customise the print settings in order to embellish your documents.

Covers

Chapter Seven

Connecting a printer

The are several options for printing files from your Psion Series 5.

For most people, the easiest way to print from the Series 5 is likely to be to connect it to a parallel-port printer using the Psion printer lead, which is available from Psion outlets. It plugs into the Series 5's port at the back of the computer and to the printer's parallel port. In order not to drain power from the Series 5's batteries, the printer end of the lead requires a 9-volt battery (Duracell MN1604).

Whichever, method you choose, the remote link must be switched off (select Ctrl+L from the System screen).

Other alternatives are :

- to use the docking lead supplied and an adapter to print to a serial printer

- to print via PsiWin2 directly to your PC

- to print via the IrDA Infra Red port

Configuring the computer

When configuring your Series 5 for printing, it is possible to set global values which will normally apply to all printing, but also local values which will apply only to the program you are using. Therefore, you could set the computer to print Word documents to one type of printer, and Agenda documents to another.

Refer to Chapter Four for information on setting the global values.

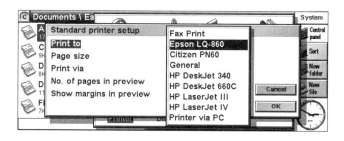

Local setup

Each Series 5 program which is capable of printing can be configured to print to a different printer if required.

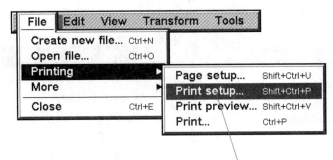

| To set the printing options for a particular program, start the program and open the menu bar. Go to File>Printing>Print setup.

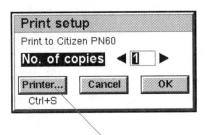

2 In the Print Setup dialog, touch the Printer button or press Ctrl+S.

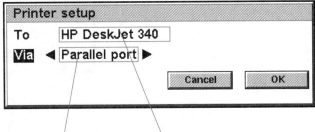

3 In the top panel, select the name of the printer you are using, and in the lower panel select the port you wish to print to.

...contd

There are initially six drivers pre-programmed into the Series 5. In due course, others will be available on disk which can be installed into the Series 5.

 If you need to buy a new printer, rather than using one you already have, it makes sense to buy one to match one of the pre-installed printer drivers.

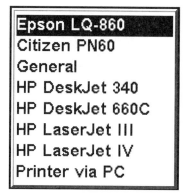

The General option will output only text to most printers. This will not include layout or highlights such as italicised text.

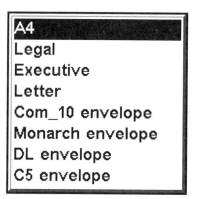

The Series 5 will support several paper sizes, including some envelope sizes. Select the correct size and touch the OK button to confirm the selections. Ensure your printer is capable of handling these sizes.

Other methods of printing

If your printer is not listed in the Print Setup menu, you will either have to wait until the correct printer driver becomes available, or look for another method.

The *Printer via PC* option will print via PsiWin to the printer connected to your PC. This solution is satisfactory, but can scarcely be regarded as being a solution in keeping with the portability of the Series 5 computer. This involves connecting your Series 5 to your PC via the docking cable supplied.

A slightly convoluted method is to export documents in a format that one of your PC programs will understand. In general, Word documents can export as text which will be able to be read by most PC-based word-processors. Data files can also be exported as text, and the spreadsheets are readable by many PC-based spreadsheets.

Exporting text from Word to a PC-based word-processor will enable you to continue working on the document at your desk and use some of the features of the desktop version not available in the Series 5.

Printing a document

Once the correct printer driver has been selected, enter Ctrl+P to open a dialog asking for the number of copies you require. Press Enter or touch the Print button to print the document.

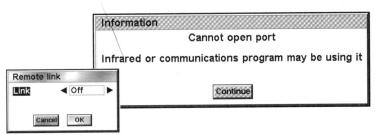

Failure to close the remote link will result in the above message. To close the link, go to the System screen and enter Ctrl+L. From the top panel of the dialog, select Off.

Customising print settings

Although basic printing can be achieved quite easily, the Series 5 has a wide range of print settings which can be customised in order to enhance your printed documents.

Touching the Print button on the right-hand toolbar will open a print preview screen which will show what the document will look like on paper.

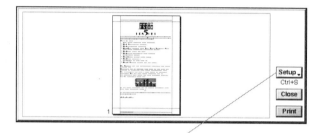

On the right are buttons to cancel or continue with the printing process, and above these is the Setup button. Selecting this leads to a menu, with the Page option at the top of the list. Selecting Page leads to a dialog box where further options related to page layout may be selected.

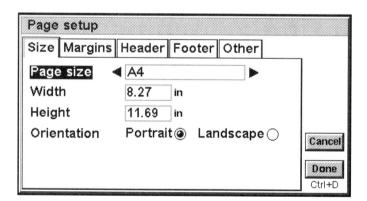

The first tab is 'Size' and the main use for this is to change from portrait (with the long side of the paper vertical) to landscape (with the long side of the paper horizontal) orientation. You can also change the paper size, including entering non-standard sizes.

...contd

The Margins tab offers the user the choice of entering margins. Unless you really know what you're doing, it's probably best to leave these settings alone.

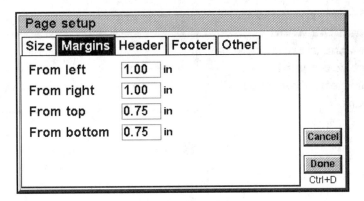

The third tab relates to the header. A header is something which will be automatically printed at the top of every page, and may include the chapter title, page number or any other heading appropriate to the page.

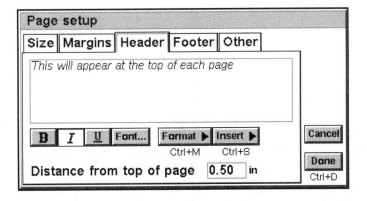

HANDY TIP

Parts of the header text can be selected and effects applied to them.

To create a header, type the phrase in the box. Effects like emboldening and underlining can be selected from this dialog, but touching the Font button will open another dialog.

...contd

 Effects can be applied to a part of the header. Touch the wand over the start of the part you wish to mark, and drag it to the end.

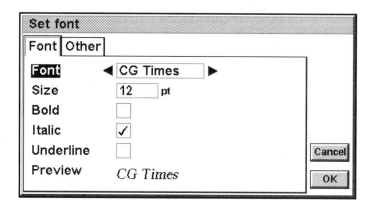

The font style (which will be determined by the type of printer you have connected) can be selected here, as can the size of the font. Bold text, italics and underlining can also be selected from this dialog and will be applied to either the whole header or a marked selection.

Touching the Other tab offers further effects.

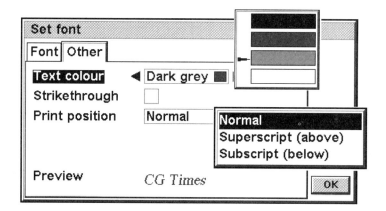

You may choose to have the text in one of four colours, which may be selected from the colour chart. You may also choose to have the text ruled through (Strikethrough), and whether to have part or all of the header as superscript (above the line) or subscript (below the line).

Touch the OK button to confirm the selection.

...contd

The *Format* button leads to a menu offering a choice of borders and colours, alignment and tab positions.

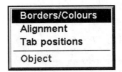

Borders/Colours offers the option of placing a frame or part of a frame around the contents of the header.

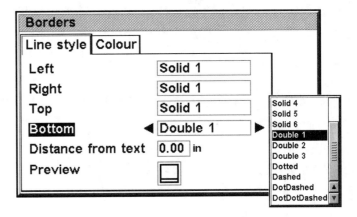

The header may be surrounded by 13 different lines, in any of four colours. Each is selected from the panels in the usual way.

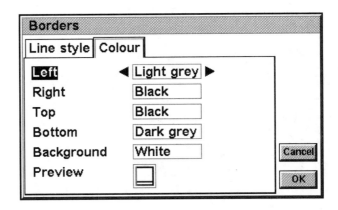

The *Alignment* option leads to a simple dialog offering the choice of aligning the contents of the header either to the left, centre or right.

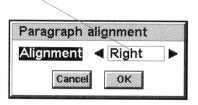

The *Tab positions* option enables you to alter the position of the header text by using tabs.

The last option of the *Format* menu is *Object;* this will not be available until an object is placed in the header.

The last button on the Header card, *Insert,* leads to a menu which will insert one or more of a variety of items. The selected item will be inserted at the position of the cursor in the Header dialog.

Enters the file name in the header

Leads to a dialog enabling you to select an object from another Series 5 application such as Sketch

Enters the current page number

Enters the total number of pages in the document being printed

Enters the current time

Enters the current date

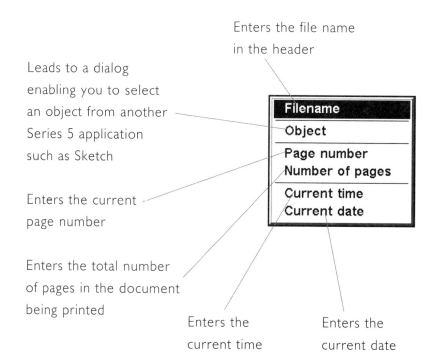

...contd

Finally, you may enter the distance the header will be printed from the top of the page.

When all of the options have been selected, touch the Done button to confirm the selections. Cancel will exit the dialogs without changing any of the settings.

Just as the header can be defined, so can a footer. A footer is exactly the same as the header, except it goes at the foot of the page.

HANDY TIP

Be selective with the effects when using both a header and a footer: don't overwhelm the page with too much information.

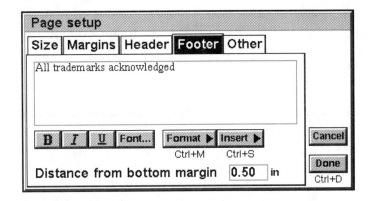

The options are identical to designing the header, and the same features may be incorporated.

The last tab on the Page Setup dialog is *Other,* which gives you the opportunity to choose the start number for automatic page-numbering in the header or footer. This feature is useful if you're producing a large piece of work and have chosen to produce the work in separate files.

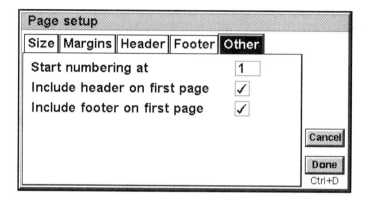

The other choices are the options to include or not include a header and/or footer on the first page.

When all of the options have been entered, touch the Done button to confirm the changes or Cancel to exit without changing any of the settings already present.

Chapter Eight

In-built applications

In this chapter, you'll learn about the major applications built into the Series 5 computer.

Overview

The Series 5 is supplied with 12 ready-to-run applications programmed into the computer's memory.

Most of the applications produce their own files, although many can accept data from other applications.

There now follows a brief introduction and outline of the most useful features, followed by a tutorial for the most important applications.

Not all of the features for every application are discussed, but merely those which are the most likely to be needed by the novice.

The main applications can be accessed from the icon bar at the bottom of the screen...

...whilst the less important applications are accessed by touching the Extras button at the right of the icon bar, which opens an on-screen icon bar containing the other programs.

The first time one of the applications is started, it will load a blank document or file. In future, touching one of the program icons will load the last file it used. If, however, the last file it used is no longer available because it has been moved or deleted, it will load a blank document.

Common keyboard shortcuts

Many of the applications have some common features which may be accessed in the same way. It is worth remembering some of the keyboard shortcuts.

Ctrl+N will create a new file. First a dialog will be displayed, into which the user must enter the file name. You may also choose where to place the file, although the default is to place it in the current System screen.

Ctrl+S will save the current file with the last file name used.

Shift+Ctrl+S will open a dialog in which you may either save the current file with a new file name and/or change the location where the file is saved.

Ctrl+R will revert to the saved version. This means that any changes to the current document will be lost and the version currently saved will be reloaded.

Ctrl+E will close and save the current file.

Ctrl+P will print the current file.

Ctrl+M will zoom in, whilst **Shift+Ctrl+M** will zoom out.

Word

Word is a full-featured word-processor which you will find extremely useful for composing any text document, from simple notes, to letters, to presentations with graphics.

From the System screen, enter Ctrl+N, or touch the New File button on the right-hand toolbar to create a new document. Either give the document a new name or leave the default name (which will be Word). Touch the OK button or press Enter to start the program.

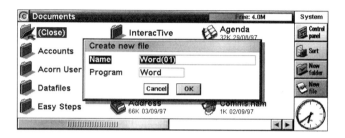

At the top of the screen will be the toolbar, which contains a number of shortcuts to commonly used features.

If the toolbar at the top is not visible, Shift+Ctrl+T will display it. It's worth keeping the top toolbar on-screen, as it contains most of the frequently used functions.

By default, the text will be 10 pt Times New Roman aligned with the left margin. The functions on the top toolbar will alter the text and add various effects.

Touching a button on the toolbar will open a menu, and touching the required item on the menu will select it. The selected style will either be applied to a marked area or to the text entered after the current cursor position.

When beginning a major piece of work, it's a good idea to spend a little time defining the styles you want to use for the body text and any titles.

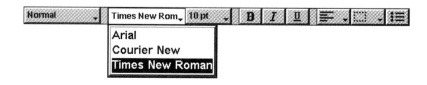

To mark a piece of text, touch the wand on the screen at the start of the piece of text you wish to mark, and either drag the wand to the end of the section you wish to mark or touch the wand at the end of the section whilst holding down Shift.

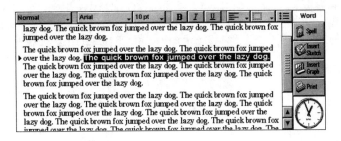

You may mix these if you really must! Use these effects sparingly to highlight a single word or phrase.

Font style. The button on the left will initially contain the word Normal – referring to the text style. Touch the button and a drop-down menu will appear containing three additional preset styles. The styles supplied may be altered at any time, including the font name and size, alignment and emphasis. Any text which uses that style in the document will take on the alterations. Additional styles may be added, in which case they will appear on the menu.

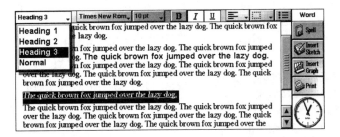

Font name. The Series 5 has three in-built display fonts: Arial, Courier and Times. The font is initially set to Times New Roman.

Font size. Font sizes are measured in points (pt). Text is initially set to 10 pt, which is a good size for body text. However, you may reduce it to 4 pt or increase it to 50 pt from this menu.

Emphasis. The next three buttons determine any font emphasis. Touching the **B** button will embolden the text, **I** will italicise it and **U** will underline it.

Alignment. When you first enter text, it will be aligned on the left of the page. The next button allows you to alter this. Central alignment is suitable for titles, and will keep the text centred even if its size is subsequently changed. Right alignment will push the text to the right so that the right-hand edge of the text will be aligned with the right-hand margin. Fully justified alignment will add extra spaces between the words so that the left and right margins are straight. (The highlighted paragraph below is fully justified.)

All of these effects can be entered in two ways. For example, you can touch the required effect button, type the text required for that style, then change to another style, and so on. The alternative method is the one that seems preferred by word-processor operators: enter the text as is, then go back to add the fancy titles and layout.

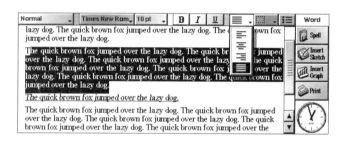

Box. This feature will place a box around a piece of text or place horizontal lines above and/or below lines of text. The boxes which are available in different line widths are suitable for highlighting small pieces of text, whilst the horizontal lines are useful for creating tables.

Bullets. Unlike the other buttons on the top toolbar, the final button does not open a menu but will place a bullet at the start of a paragraph and indent the rest of the paragraph. This feature is useful for emphasising points.

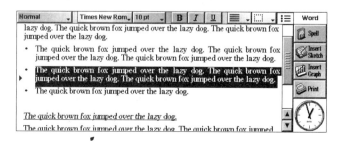

Other frequently used features

There are many features in Word, some very advanced, but the most frequently used are likely to be spell-checking, Search & Replace, and Cut, Copy and Paste. If you don't attempt to understand any of the other features, you should at least learn how to use these.

Spell-checking. Before looking at what the spell-checker will do, it might be useful to point out what it will not do. First, it is not a grammar checker; it will not look at the context of words. The sentence "The ball is over their," for example, would be not be queried because none of the words are misspelt. Of course, the sentence uses 'their' when it should be 'there', but the computer wouldn't know this. Second, just because the computer queries a word, it does not necessarily mean that the word is misspelt, but that the computer doesn't recognise it. However, such words can be added to the dictionary so they are not queried in future.

Make sure that any words added to the dictionary are correctly spelt.

To spell-check a document, either touch the Spell button on the right-hand toolbar (Ctrl+T will display the right toolbar if it is absent), or type Ctrl+L.

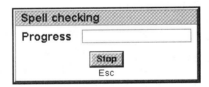

To stop the spell-checker always checking from the start of the document, mark a piece of text by dragging the wand over it. Only the marked text will be checked.

The computer will 'read' through the text. When it finds something it doesn't recognise, it displays a dialog which shows the whole phrase containing the queried word and five touch buttons.

Unrecognised word "jumpd"

...dog. The quick brown fox jumpd over the lazy dog. The ...

Stop	Skip	Skip all	Add to dictionary	Correct
Esc	Space	Ctrl+I	Ctrl+A	Enter

Touching the Correct button will open a new dialog where the computer may offer some alternative words, or you may have to try typing it again.

Spell: Correcting a word

Word to correct: jumpd

Correction   jumped

Suggestions   jumped

Cancel	Correct all	Correct
Esc	Ctrl+A	Enter

When complete, a message will appear for a short while, stating how many unknown words were found.

Find and Replace. This feature will enable you to automatically search for a word or phrase and optionally replace it with another word or phrase. If, after entering a long piece of text, you find that you have used the word 'palmtop' rather a lot, you can replace some occurrences with the word 'computer'. Alternatively, if you have written a document about, say, Kendle House, and you later find that its name is actually Kendale House, you can perform a global search and replace so that every occurrence of 'Kendle' is replaced with 'Kendale'.

Beware when searching for a word which occasionally appears at the start of a sentence. If the replacing word does not begin with a capital letter, then you will lose the capital letter at the beginning of a sentence which opened with the search word.

The Replace dialog is summoned by touching the menu icon on the left toolbar and selecting Edit>Find>Replace or using the keyboard shortcut Ctrl+H. The dialog opens with the word at the current cursor position in the top text box. You must enter a search word or phrase and a replace word or phrase into the dialog. To begin the search, touch OK or press Enter. The search will start at the current cursor position and will either search towards the start of the document or towards the end of the document, depending on which of the two buttons (Up and Down) has been selected.

...contd

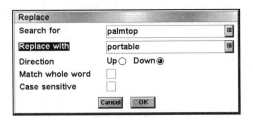

HANDY TIP To search the whole document, press Shift+Fn+Up arrow to move the cursor to the start of the document, and ensure the Down button is selected.

When the first occurrence of the search word is found, a new dialog opens, and you have the choice of changing that occurrence (in which case the same dialog will reappear when the next occurrence is found), or of replacing every occurrence of the word or phrase. There is also the option of aborting the search.

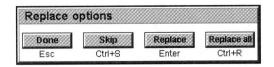

Other options include specifying whether the search should be case-sensitive. If this option is ticked, then the computer will look for an exact match, including capital letters.

Edit menu (Cut, Copy and Paste). This feature enables you to easily copy or move text. The Edit button, (the second button from the top on the left-hand toolbar) leads to a menu with three options: Cut, Copy and Paste. Mark a piece of text by dragging the wand over it so that it is highlighted.

HANDY TIP If you don't like dragging the wand over the screen, touch the wand at the start of the section you wish to mark, then hold down the Shift key and touch the wand at the end of the section you want marked.

Unlike many other word-processors, marking a piece of text and pressing Delete does *not* copy the text into the clipboard.

Open the Edit menu and touch Cut. The piece of text will be removed from the document but placed into a special area of the computer's memory called the clipboard. Touch the wand on another part of the document (or indeed, another document), open the Edit menu, and touch Paste. The text from the clipboard will be inserted into the document at the current cursor position.

Copy is the same as Cut except that the marked text is not removed from the document.

Once a piece of text is in the clipboard, it will remain there until another piece of text is copied into it. Therefore, the contents of the clipboard can be pasted into a document as many times as you like.

Sketch

The second button on the right-hand toolbar allows you to place a sketch at the current cursor position. Touch the Insert Sketch button and a screen similar to that of Sketch will open. (Refer to the Sketch topic, starting on page 116.) After creating your Sketch, touch on the Done button at the top of the screen.

 You can use Cut, Copy and Paste to move your sketch, and you can align it, just like text.

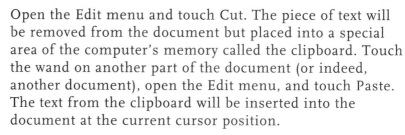

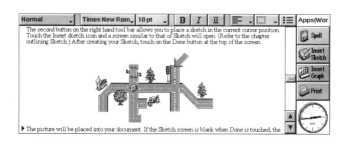

The picture will be placed into your document. If the Sketch screen is blank when Done is touched, the Word document will not be altered. Double-touching the picture will take you back to the screen used to create it so that it may be edited. Touching the picture and then pressing Delete will remove it.

Insert Graph

Touching the Insert Graph button takes you to a screen similar to that of Sheet. (Refer to the Sheet topic, starting on page 100.) After creating your spreadsheet and producing a graph from it, touch on the Done button at the top of the screen. The picture will be placed into your document.

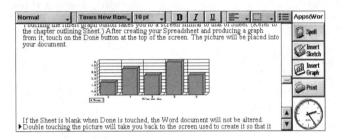

If the Sheet is blank when Done is touched, the Word document will not be altered. Double-touching the picture will take you back to the screen used to create it so that it may be edited. Touching the picture and then pressing Delete will remove it.

Tutorial

One of the tasks you can perform to get familiar with the word-processor is to create a letter in the way most word-processor operators would: enter the text as is and then go back to add the fancy titles and layout.

1 Having created a new document, type in your address. Normally your address would go on the right, but leave it on the left for the moment. Press Enter once at the end of each line and twice after the postcode.

2 Next, enter the date. Don't use abbreviations.

3 Enter the address of the person to whom you wish to send your letter. Again, press Enter once at the end of each line and twice after the postcode.

...contd

4 Now type in a reference. If you want to include a reference number, you could use the small 'o' commonly used when the word 'Number' is abbreviated to 'N°'. To access this character, touch the menu icon at the top on the left toolbar and select Insert>Special character. A dialog will open, listing all of the extra characters which are programmed into the Series 5 but are not directly available from the keyboard.

HANDY TIP

If you've got an analogue clock in the bottom right corner of the screen, touch it to change it to a digital clock which will have today's date under the time.

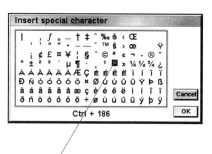

5 Touch the wand on character 186 and touch OK. The character will be inserted at the current cursor position, which should be after the letter 'N'.

6 Now type the salutation ('Dear Sir', 'Dear Janet', etc.). Press Enter twice.

7 Enter a few lines of text for the body of the letter. At the end of the letter, press Enter and type 'Yours sincerely' or 'Yours faithfully', followed by Enter four or five times (to create the space where you would eventually sign the letter). Finally, type in your name.

8 Now the text has been entered, return to the top of the letter to alter the layout. Your address would normally be positioned at the top left of the page. To move it there, drag the wand over your address to mark it, then touch the align button on the toolbar at the top of the screen.

...contd

Shift+ Ctrl+W will perform a count of the words in the document and temporarily display the number in the top right of the screen.

9 From the drop-down menu displayed, touch the right-align option. While the text is marked, you could try changing the font to, say, Arial.

10 The reference which was entered before the salutation would normally go after, and is often centred. Mark the line of text and centre it first by touching the align button on the top toolbar and selecting the centre option. While it is still marked, touch the Edit button and select Cut from the menu. Touch the screen just after the salutation, open the Edit menu and touch Paste.

Printing your document

The Control panel, which is accessed from the System screen, contains an icon for printer setup. Entering printer details there will relate to all printing, but each Series 5 program which is capable of printing can be configured to print to a different printer if required. To set the printing options for Word, do the following:

1 Start Word and open the menu bar. Select File>Printing> Print setup>Printer. Enter the name of the printer and/or the port you wish to print to. Touch OK or press Enter on each of the dialogs to confirm the choices.

2 When you are ready to print, touch the Print button on the right-hand toolbar or press Ctrl+P. A dialog will open, asking you for the number of copies you require and how many pages from a multi-page document you require. When these are set, touch Print or press Enter.

Data

A database is a collection of organised information. The information is held in records, with each record holding information about one 'thing' (e.g., for a database about cars, each record would contain information about one car). Each record is divided into fields. Using the same example of a database about cars, the fields might be Make, Model, Fuel consumption, etc.

Once the data has been entered, it can be sorted into almost any order you wish and searched to locate a specific record or group of records.

You could use the Data application to keep an inventory of all your valuables. The fields might include name of product, date of purchase and serial number. In the event of an insurance claim, this type of information could prove invaluable.

The Data application in the Series 5 has a blank data file for an address book, with space for the name, telephone number, email address and other relevant information. It is probably the most common use for a database on a personal computer, but you could build a database on almost anything you want, from the E numbers found in foods to a coin collection.

Although the address book may be completed 'as is', you might prefer to alter or remove some of the field names or 'labels', as they are referred to in the software.

Creating a new file

From the System screen, touch the wand once on the New File icon on the toolbar on the right of the screen, give the new file a name (e.g. AddressBook) and set the Program field to 'Data'. Alternatively, you could press Ctrl+N, or select it from the menu: File>Create new file.

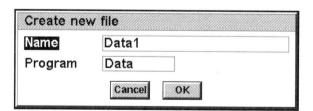

This will load the default document (an address book) containing 8 field names, but zero records.

...contd

Altering the labels

If you wish to remove, rename, reorder or in any way change the labels given to you, touch the Menu button on the left-hand toolbar or press Menu and select Tools> Change labels.

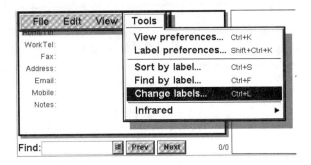

HANDY TIP

In keeping with the other labels already present, end any new labels with a colon (:).

A dialog will open, listing the current labels. If you wish to add a label, touch the Add Label button and a second dialog will open. Enter the name you wish to use for your label.

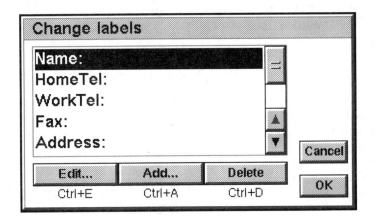

After typing in the label name, the next task is to enter the data type. The Data application can handle six different types of data. It is well worth considering what information is likely to be entered under the particular label; choose the data type appropriately.

...contd

The six data types are:

Text. Anything which contains letters must be text. This is the most widely used data type, and examples of its use include names, addresses and post codes.

Number. This means a whole number, and the only characters allowed in this field are 0–9 and the minus sign to represent a negative number. You may also set the range for the field (e.g. the highest and lowest limit). This data type should only be used if you are entering data which cannot possibly contain a fraction, e.g. Number of People.

Floating point. This is a number which includes a decimal point and fractions of a number expressed as a decimal. You may only use the characters 0–9 in this field, the minus sign to represent a negative number and the full stop to represent a decimal point. Use this data type for numbers which could include fractions, e.g. shoe sizes.

Date. Only dates are allowed in this field and take the format dd/mm/yyyy (e.g. 09/07/1954 means 9th July 1954). If you're entering information about people, it's much better to enter their date of birth rather than their age.

Yes/No. The value of a Yes/No field can either be Yes or No.

Memo. This is a text file which may have an unlimited number of characters. You are only allowed a maximum of 16 memo fields per data file. If you want to include some fairly lengthy descriptions, use this data type.

When creating new labels, after entering the name, choose the file type and touch OK or press Enter.

If you wish to delete a label, touch the label to highlight it and then touch the Delete button or press the Delete key.

You may change existing labels by touching the Edit button to open a dialog. Make the changes you wish and touch the OK button or press Enter.

If you have records which use a label which you subsequently delete, you will lose all the items of data associated with that label.

...contd

If you have added or amended labels, you may wish to place them in a particular order. Open the menu and go to Tools>Label preferences.

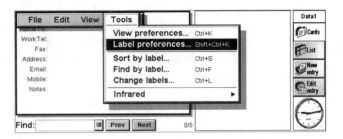

Touch the label you wish to move to highlight it, then touch the wand on either the Move Up button or the Move Down button.

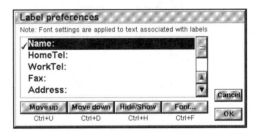

While you are in that dialog you may also make changes to the font, including the size.

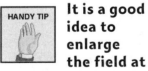

It is a good idea to enlarge the field at the top. In the case of the address book, this will probably be the person's name.

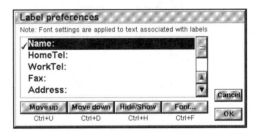

These changes may be applied to any field or fields you wish. Touch the label to highlight it, then touch the Font button.

Choose the font name and size and any other effects you wish. Touch OK or press Enter when finished. The font effect applies to the data only, and not to the actual labels.

Once you have completed the labels and they are set up as you want them, you can begin entering the records. You can at any time go back and re-edit the labels, although if a label is deleted any information associated with that label will be lost.

Entering records

Touch the New Entry button on the right-hand toolbar and a dialog opens listing the labels, with a space alongside each in which you can enter the data.

Touch the space alongside each label and type in the data. Then touch each field (or press the down arrow key) to move the cursor to the field into which you wish to enter the data. You do not have to use every field in every record, as an unused field will not appear on the record.

You will not be allowed to use inappropriate data in a field – e.g. if you have declared a field as having number data, you will not be able to enter letters.

When a record is complete, touch the wand on the Save button and another blank record card will be displayed for you to enter your next record.

You may continue to add and amend records at any time. Touch the Close button when you have finished entering data.

Editing a record

You may change a record by first displaying it and then touching the Edit entry button on the right-hand toolbar. You may then touch the wand on the item or items you wish to change and alter or retype the entry. Touching the Save button or pressing Ctrl+S will save the changes.

Views

There are basically two views in Data. Normally you will see the individual records shown as cards...

...but touching the List button on the right-hand toolbar will change the display to a list.

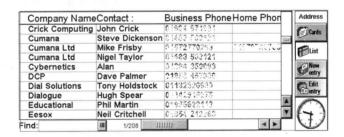

Touching the Cards button will restore the 'card index' appearance.

Optionally, you may have a 'browser' on the same screen as the card index and specify how much of the screen the card will take. The remainder will be occupied by the browser, which is a list of the items in the first field.

...contd

The items in the list can be touched upon to display that particular record, or scrolled through using the vertical scroll bar.

The browser may be displayed by opening the menus and going to Tools>View Preferences.

Sorting

The records may be sorted into order by any field or fields you choose. Actually you can choose up to three fields to sort the data. Open the menus and select Tools>Sort by label.

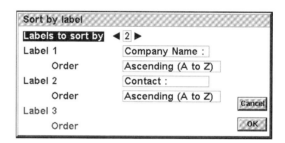

A dialog will open, and the first entry must be the number of fields you wish to sort by. You may enter 1, 2 or 3. Click on the field alongside Label 1 and choose the first label, which will probably be Name or Surname. You may also specify if you want the order to be ascending or descending. If you are sorting Surnames into alphabetical order, it might be worth having a second label to sort for forenames. This will ensure the people will be ordered by their surname, but those with the same surname will be 'sub-sorted' into order by their first name.

Searching

Probably the most common task you'll carry out on your address book is to search for a name, a telephone number, an email address etc. The easiest way to search is to type in what you're looking for alongside the word Find: and press Enter.

The program will search through the whole file for occurrences of the word or phrase you entered, initially in all fields. When it has searched through the whole file, it will display the number of matches at the bottom centre of the screen. The first record containing the matched search string will be displayed, and if the Card browser is on screen, it will list as many records as possible by the first field. If there is more than one record that matches the search string, you may touch the Previous and Next buttons to see the others. If the Card browser is available, simply touch the name in one of the boxes.

You may restrict the number of fields the software searches by opening the menus and selecting Tools>Find by label. You may deselect any of the labels by simply touching the label. Touching it again reselects it. The search will now be only on the labels you chose rather than all of them.

...contd

Dialling

When you have found a record, you may automatically dial the telephone number (if one exists), providing the data file 'knows' that it is a phone number.

You may have several fields set up to dial telephone numbers, e.g. Business phone, Home phone, Facsimile, etc.

Open the menus and select Tools>Change labels, and you'll see a list of the labels in the data file. Touch the one containing the telephone number to highlight it, then select Edit>Options. The top option on the dialog now displayed (Search label for phone numbers when dialling) should be ticked.

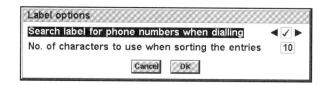

Close down the top two dialogs (Options and Edit) by touching the OK buttons, and if necessary select another telephone number field so that it too may be set up in the same way.

If you frequently travel abroad, it might be worth including the international code in your address book.

Having found the required record, press Fn+Menu to display a dialog containing all the fields selected as containing a telephone number. To dial a number, select the one required from the list (if there is more than one).

Hold the Series 5's speaker about 150 mm from the mouthpiece of the phone and touch Dial (or press Space) to dial the exact number shown, or touch Dial out (or press Enter) to add an outside line prefix as determined by the settings in the Control panel.

Ready-made data files

There are several data files available from a variety of sources, including the Internet. Some are the result of a great many hours' work, and so can be quite expensive to purchase.

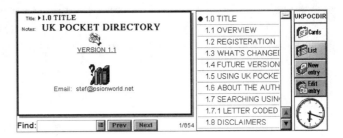

Some, on the other hand, are either free or almost free. One shareware data file is the UK Pocket Directory by Stefan Smith, and contains a wealth of information on all manner of topics, from Internet site addresses to what to do if you lose your Series 5. The topics are not all computer-related; there is also information about tourist information centres, police, AA travel advice, air travel and building societies.

Once loaded, you may either enter a word in the Find box, or use the browser to locate the subject you require information about.

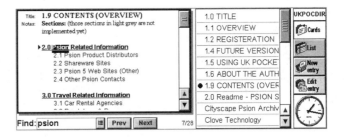

If you do use this data file, it is most important that you register so that the author can continue development.

The address is at the back of the book.

Sheet

A spreadsheet is usually used for financial accounting, and will be useful for keeping track of your bank account(s) and other financial dealings.

The spreadsheet is a page which is divided up into boxes called cells. Each cell has a unique name taken from the letters at the top of each column and the numbers alongside each row. When a new sheet is opened, the current cell (the one with the marker – a black line around it) will be A1.

To enter data, type here and press Enter...

...and it appears in the current cell.

The marker can be moved by either touching the required cell or by using the arrow keys to move the marker from cell to cell. Touching a cell and dragging the wand over other cells will mark the cells, primarily for the purpose of copying.

Each cell is capable of holding a single piece of data. The most commonly used are:

- a number, whole (i.e., an integer) or real (with fractions)

- a word, phrase or letter

- a time or date

- a formula (which always begins with =)

Of them all, the formula is perhaps the most important, as it is this feature which lets the program do more than just display data, enabling it to compute the data.

...contd

Tutorial

It is easiest to explain how a spreadsheet works by example, and so unlike the previous explanations, we'll use the program to produce a multiplication table. This simple exercise will get you familiar with many of the features of spreadsheets in general, and Sheet in particular.

1 Create a new Sheet document called 'Table'. Touch the New file button on the right-hand toolbar, select the file type (Sheet) and enter the file name in the top text box.

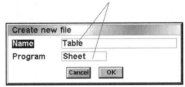

2 In cell AI place the number I. Then go to BI and enter the number 2. To create a multiplication table, those are the only numbers that need to be entered – the rest should be formulae and the first one should go into cell CI. Go to CI and enter (exactly as written) *=A I*B I* and press Enter.

HANDY TIP

To change the whole entry of a cell, simply touch the wand on the cell and retype the entry. To make an alteration, touch the wand first on the cell and then at the writable area at the top of the screen.

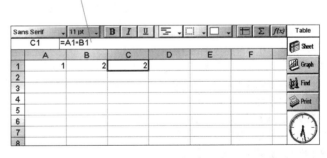

What you'll see in CI is not the formula, but the result of the calculation: 2. The clever part is that you can now change the value in cell AI or BI, and the number displayed in CI will automatically change. Try changing the number 1 in AI to a 5 and the number 2 in BI to a 3. After each number is entered, cell CI will update so that it always contains whatever is in AI multiplied by whatever is in BI.

...contd

Since this is a simple multiplication table, column A will always contain numbers ascending in steps of 1. Therefore A2 will contain the formula =A1+1. A3 will be =A2+1, A4 will be =A3+1 and so on. However...

3 Instead of typing the formula into all the cells in column A, type it just once into cell A2 (=A1 + 1) and copy it either by using Ctrl+C or by opening the Edit menu (Cut, Copy and Paste) on the left-hand toolbar and touching Copy. Now touch the wand on cell A3 and drag down as far as you wish to go. Keep the wand in column A and the cells you drag across will be highlighted.

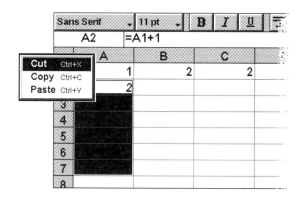

To mark a selection of cells, first touch the cell at the top left of the group of cells you wish to mark and then either drag the wand to the bottom right cell of the group you wish to mark, or hold down Shift and touch the cell at the bottom right of the group you.

4 Now paste the formula either by pressing Ctrl+V or by opening the Edit menu and touching Paste. The formula will be copied into all marked cells, although if you look, the formula will have been changed slightly for each cell.

5 Column B will always contain the same number, so in B2 enter =B1. Again, with the marker in B2, copy, touch B3, then drag down and paste the formula.

6 Finally, the formula applied to C1 will need to go into all cells in column C, so mark it, copy it, select the rest of the column and paste.

...contd

If you've done it correctly, you should have the 2 times table, starting at 1. But, by changing the number in cell B1 you can get any multiplication table you wish. You may also change the initial number by changing the value in A1, or even introduce negative numbers.

Press Esc to unmark cells.

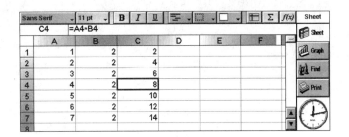

7 Save the multiplication table by pressing Ctrl+S or exit by using Ctrl+E.

Other features of Sheet

Across the top of the spreadsheet is a toolbar containing eleven buttons.

In general, these effects are best applied by first marking the cell or cells you wish to apply the effect to.

To increase or decrease the size of a row or column, touch and hold the wand on the line between the row or column labels at the top or left edge of the spreadsheet.

Font. Initially the font is set to Sans Serif. Touching this button opens a menu showing the currently available fonts. Selecting a different font will change the current cell or the marked cells.

Font size. This button leads to a menu offering a choice of font sizes. Choosing a larger font may mean that the contents of the cell may no longer fit, in which case the row-height or column-width may need to be increased.

Font effects. The B, *I* and U buttons will embolden, italicise or underline the contents of the selected cells.

Alignment. This button leads to a menu offering the choice of placing the contents of marked cells on the left, right or centre.

Cell border. Each cell or group of cells may have a border around them. The top eight choices in the menu will place either a box or a line around every marked cell. The bottom two options will place a single box around all marked cells. Most options are available in two line widths.

Colouring or outlining cells is a good way of highlighting titles or totals.

Cell colour. This will change the colour of the current cell or marked cells.

Freeze cells. Touching this button will place a dark cross line to the top and the left of the current cell. All cells above and to the left of the cross line are frozen and will not scroll. This enables you to keep certain cells, such as titles, in view.

Sum. Touching the Sum button will place a formula in the current cell which adds together all cells in the current column.

Function. This leads to a dialog offering a choice of functions.

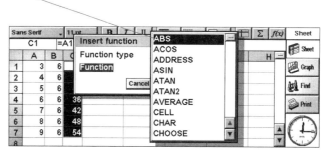

When the required function is selected, it is placed on the edit line. In most cases the function will finish with two brackets, with the cursor in between. Type in the cells you wish to calculate and press Enter.

Graphs

You may create a graph from any of the rows or columns in a spreadsheet.

Using the spreadsheet from the tutorial, touch the heading of column C to mark the whole column, then touch the Graph button on the right-hand toolbar.

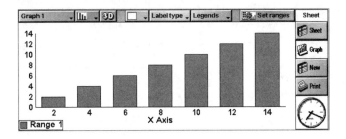

You should see a graph of the answers to the current multiplication table. In its present form, the graph is 'live', which means that if you return to the sheet (by touching the Sheet button on the right-hand toolbar), alter it and then return to the graph, it will have changed to reflect changes made in the sheet. Try changing the contents of A1 to, say, 6. Assuming B1 contains the number 2, the graph should now begin with 12. Whilst in the spreadsheet, you might also touch the header above column A to mark the whole of that column. We will use this later for a second graph.

Return to the graph and touch the New button on the right-hand toolbar.

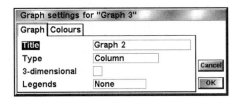

This will open a dialog for a new graph. You may select a variety of options related to the graph, but initially just give it a name. 'Graph 2' will be fine. Now touch OK or press Enter.

...contd

Double-touching the wand on the actual graph will open a dialog enabling you to make some adjustments to the graph. The dialog has three tabs, and the active tab will normally be Ranges.

The options you can choose for a graph will depend on the type of graph you are working with. For example, the marker type is only relevant for line graphs, whilst colours are only relevant for graphs with solid areas like bar and pie charts.

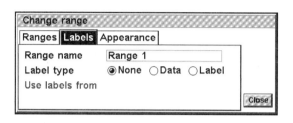

Choose the range you wish to adjust and whether or not you want the range to be displayed. Touching the Labels tab gives you the chance decide which label type you wish to have for each set of data, and Appearance enables you to choose colours and marker types for each data set.

The toolbar

At the top of the Graph screen is a toolbar with seven buttons which are used to access some of the graph options.

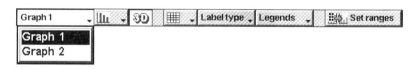

The other buttons relate only to the graph currently displayed.

Graph. The button on the left displays the current graph name. Touch the button and a drop-down menu will appear listing all current graphs. If you followed the tutorial, you will have two, the one highlighted being the one currently displayed. Touch the name of another to display that graph.

Graph symbol. Touching the graph symbol button will display a drop-down menu showing seven graph types supported in Sheet. The current type is highlighted; touching another will select that type.

3D. Touching this button will switch between a 2-dimensional display and a 3-dimensional one.

...contd

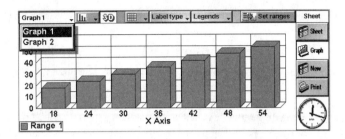

Grid. Touching the grid symbol button will display a drop-down menu showing four grids: none, horizontal, vertical or both horizontal and vertical. The current type is highlighted; touching another will select that one.

Label type. This button displays a drop-down menu offering a choice of no labels, data or normal labels. The current type is highlighted; touching another will select that type.

Legends. For each set of data displayed as a graph, you may have a legend which describes the data and applies either a colour or a marker type to each set of data. This drop-down menu provides the choice of location for the legends. Touching the legends leads to a dialog in which you may change the graph name and the colours for the text and axis.

Set Ranges. This is the last button on the top toolbar.

Touching one of the axes will display a dialog which will enable you to set the scale for the axis and several other options, including adding a label to the axis and selecting its text size and colour.

Touch the Sheet button to return to the spreadsheet.

Agenda

One of the most useful applications for a small, pocket-size computer is a personal diary. Agenda is a very powerful program which many regarded as the most useful single application on the Series 3a and 3c. Agenda on the Series 5 is even better.

Apart from appointments, you could use Agenda to keep a diary (in the traditional sense of the word, i.e. a record of your life) or even a record of your diet.

At its simplest, Agenda is a personal organiser. However, the program can control several files, which means that potentially it is several organisers, each possibly containing events related to a different subject. If necessary, the different agendas may be synchronised.

Initially the Agenda display appropriately resembles an open book.

Agenda has several views, but whichever view is first displayed, it always opens on today's page or (in the case of the Year planner) with the highlight on today's date. On the right is a toolbar with four options in addition to the title button at the top, which, as always, contains the file name. Touching it will lead to a dialog to enable you to close this and/or any other open file.

View button

The top button of the right-hand toolbar is the View button. Touching the View button opens a menu showing the various views available in Agenda.

The highlight will be on the name of the current view; touching one of the others in the list will display that view.

The **Day view** is an open book which shows hourly slots from 6am to 10pm.

Events which fall outside those times may still be entered, and the slots will expand to cater for events requiring more than a single line of description.

Not surprisingly, the **Week view** shows the whole current week. The start of the week will normally be Monday, unless you chose another day to begin the week when entering your preferences in the Control panel.

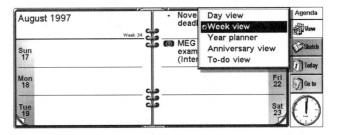

Days which contain more information than can be displayed on a particular day will inherit a small downward-pointing arrow. Touching the arrowhead will scroll the text, at which point an upward-pointing arrow will appear to enable you to scroll the text back to the start.

The **Year planner** shows the whole of the current year, with a box highlighting today's date.

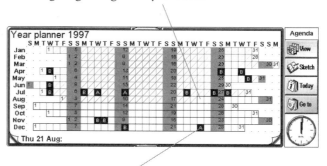

Anniversaries are shown, and touching these will display the text associated with that anniversary at the foot of the screen. Touching any day will display that date at the bottom left of the screen.

The **Anniversary view** shows four months at a time, with all the anniversaries listed for each month.

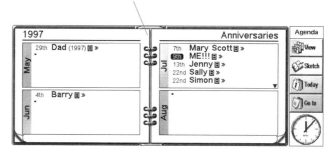

The **To-do view** lists all of the tasks in order of priority. Tasks may be crossed out when done or removed from the list.

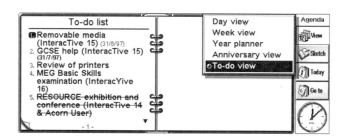

In the bottom left- and right-hand corners of each view are page turns. These look like curled-up page corners; touching one will move either to the previous page or to the next page.

Sketch

The second button on the right-hand toolbar allows you to place a sketch in the current cursor position. Touch the Sketch button and a screen similar to that of Sketch will open. After creating your sketch, touch the Done button at the top of the screen.

The picture will be placed into your document. If the Sketch screen is blank when Done is touched, the Agenda document will not be altered. Double-touching the picture will take you back to the screen used to create the drawing so that it may be edited. Touching the picture and then pressing Delete will remove it.

Today

Regardless of which view is displayed, touching the Today button will always highlight or display today's date. If the To-do view is displayed, it will change to the Day view.

If you prefer to use the keyboard, Ctrl+G followed by Enter will always take you back to today's page.

Go to

Touching the Go-to button will display a dialog containing the currently selected date. Enter a preferred date and press Enter to jump to that date.

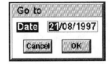

Entering appointments in Agenda

You may enter daily appointments in either the Day or Week views. Entries in the day or week view can have their start time and duration or end time specified. To enter an appointment, do the following:

1 Touch the wand on the approximate time you wish to begin your entry (i.e., if you wish to enter an appointment on a particular date at 12.30 am, go to the date, and touch the wand on 12.00 pm).

**The Tools>
Entry
preferences
menu leads
to dialogs in which
you may specify
certain default
values, including
the standard
duration of an
appointment.**

2 When you begin typing, a dialog entitled 'Create new day entry' will open containing the text entered so far. Continue to enter the text. If the start time is incorrect, you may alter it. Appointments are initially 1 hour long, but you may alter this or enter a finish time.

**To delete
an entry,
touch it
once and
then press Delete.
You'll be asked to
confirm before the
entry is removed.**

3 Alternatively, you may not want the entry to be timed. If this is the case, touch 'Timed entry' on the dialog and it will simply be entered as a note.

4 When you've finished, touch OK or press Enter. If you selected a timed entry, the duration will be marked on the view.

You may make several alterations to the entry by touching the More... button on the dialog. This will open a tabbed dialog with the Alarm tab selected. There are four areas in which you may make alterations to the appearance of your Agenda entry: Text, Details, Alarm and Other.

Setting an alarm

1 Go to the Alarm tab and select 'Has alarm' by touching the box alongside so that it now contains a tick. The other items on the card will now be available, and in these you may enter either the time you wish the alarm to sound, or the amount of time by which the alarm should precede the event.

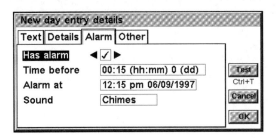

2 You may also select the type of alarm from the list supplied, which could include ones you recorded with the record application. (See the 'Record' topic on pages 122–123.)

Set your alarms to sound at a particular time of day – at a time you know you will normally have your Series 5 with you.

When you return to either the Day view or the Week view, the entry will have an alarm symbol alongside it. The alarm will sound at the specified time even if your Series 5 is switched off.

Further alterations include selecting a font, a font size, adding emphasis such as emboldening and setting a letter code for the type of entry.

1 Touch the Text tab; the dialog opens with the text entered (which can be altered if required).

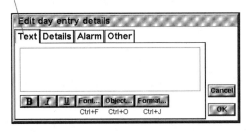

...contd

Start as you mean to continue. Decide what the entry symbols are and stick to them. Use the Tools> Entry preferences dialogs to set up as many default values as possible.

2 Highlight a part of the text, then add effects like underline, italic or bold using the buttons at the bottom of the tab. The Font button leads to another dialog in which you can select the style and size of the font.

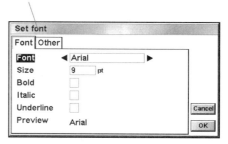

3 Click OK to return to the previous dialog.

4 You may also include an object to go with your entry from this dialog. An object may be a picture, a text file, a spreadsheet or a recorded sound, possibly a voice note. Touch the Object button and a dialog opens, asking you to select the program from which the object will be generated.

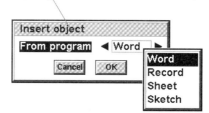

5 Select a program to create your embedded object.

6 Once the object has been created, press the Done button and the object will be embedded into the Agenda entry.

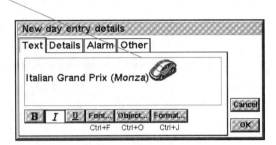

7 To re-edit an object, touch the object in the dialog and it will be opened in the application that was used to create it.

8 The Format button will open a dialog which will enable you to carry out some fine-tuning on the positioning of the object, but only if the object was created in either Sketch or Sheet.

Entry symbols

Each entry may be given its own entry code, e.g. A – Anniversary, B – Birthday, E – Event, R – Religious, etc.

Events

Entries made in the Year planner will be for a whole day, and are referred to as an event. They will carry the entry symbol E, unless you changed it in the Entry preferences dialog. Events will usually be birthdays and anniversaries, and this is a good project to get you started: enter the names and birthdays of all your friends and family.

Like other entries, events can have an alarm attached to them, which can be programmed to sound a specified number of days in advance and at a particular time.

Sketch

While the vast majority of the functions of most of the other programs can be carried out solely from the keyboard, Sketch relies heavily on the touch wand.

Sketch is a bitmap editor, which basically means it allows you to colour the individual dots on the screen – the picture elements or 'pixels'. This is done with the aid of some tools which may seem strangely familiar.

Try to keep the selection rectangle as close to the object as possible. What you're actually doing is marking an area of the screen.

When run, Sketch displays a toolbox on the right of the screen, which can be hidden and revealed with Ctrl+T. In addition to the 12 tools, there is a palette and line-width selector. To select a tool or to change colour or line-width, simply touch the required button on the toolbox. If you prefer not to have the toolbox on-screen, all the options may be selected by touching the menu button on the left toolbar and selecting Tools>Drawing tools.

If your drawing is made up of a number of parts, draw each part at the edge of the screen and then drag it to the required position when you're sure it's correct.

Select. This is the main editing tool and is roughly equivalent to marking text in Word. Once the Select tool has been chosen, touch the screen near to an object and drag a rectangle over the object to envelope it.

Remove the wand from the screen and the selected area will have a eight 'blobs' or nodes around it. Touching another part of the screen will deselect the area.

...contd

The nodes on the corners will allow you to alter the size both vertically and horizontally, whilst the nodes on the edges only allow re-sizing in one direction.

Once an area is selected, you can carry out any of a number of operations. If you touch the menu button on the left toolbar and go to Transform, you will see that it's possible to flip the selected area either vertically or horizontally, rotate it, make the background transparent or opaque, or reverse the colours.

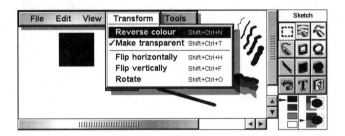

Choosing opaque or transparent background may also be selected from the bottom right of the toolbar when in Select mode.

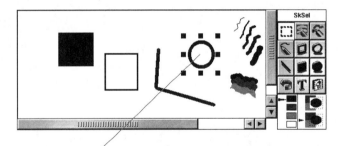

Touching the wand in the centre of a selected area will enable you to drag it around the screen and reposition it. Touching one of the nodes will allow you to stretch or shrink the area in any direction.

Rubber. If you make a mistake, select the rubber and carefully erase the error by rubbing the wand over the parts that need to be removed. Once selected, you can choose one of four rubber sizes from the panel below and to the right of the toolbox.

Airbrush. This is used like a mini spray-gun and is for shading. Choose the size of the spray and the colour from the panels below the toolbox. Careful use of light colours with darker colours inside can produce some good effects.

 Freehand pencil. Select the pencil and draw on the screen with the wand in much the same way as you would draw with a conventional pencil on paper. You may select the line-thickness and colour from the panels below the toolbox.

 Outline rectangle. As with most computer art programs, to draw a rectangle you select two diagonally opposite corners. Place the wand on one corner and drag to the other. Before drawing the rectangle, you may select the line-thickness and colour from the panels below the toolbox.

 Outline ellipse. This is used in the same way as the outline rectangle tool (by defining two diagonally opposite points), except that the final shape will be an ellipse instead of a rectangle. As with the rectangle, you may select the line-thickness and colour from the panels below the toolbox.

 Straight line. To draw straight lines, select this tool, touch the wand on the place you wish the line to start, and drag the wand to the place you wish to end the line. When you remove the wand from the screen, the line will be left.

 Filled rectangle. This is identical to the outline rectangle, except that it creates a filled rectangle in the colour selected from the panel below the toolbox.

 Filled ellipse. This is identical to the outline ellipse, except that it creates a filled ellipse in the colour selected from the panel below the toolbox.

 Undo. When touched, this tool will undo the previous action. The program stores the last five actions, so only the last five can be undone.

Text. Selecting this tool will open a dialog into which you may enter some text in the selected font style, with emphasis if required. Several lines of text may be entered, although you must press Enter at the end of each line. Once the text has been pasted onto the drawing, no further changes to the font style can be made. When the text has been placed on the drawing, it can be dragged into position or scaled using one of the eight nodes around it.

 Clipart library. Sketch is supplied with a clipart library containing 72 separate images.

When the clipart icon is touched, a window showing the first 24 images is displayed. The scroll bars can be used to reveal the others. When the image you require is displayed, touch it with the wand and it will be placed at the top left of the drawing area. Use the wand to drag it to the required position.

As several of the functions use the top left of the screen, it's a good idea to keep that area as clear as possible.

Other key features

There are several other features which will be useful when creating a drawing, but the most useful are Zoom, Cut, Copy and Paste.

Zoom. The magnifying glass on the left toolbar will set your drawing to three levels of magnification: 1:1, 2:1 and 4:1. This is useful for fine detailing, as the pixels are much larger and can be adjusted with a great deal more accuracy.

Cut, Copy and Paste. Once an area of the screen has been selected with the Select tool, it can be edited in a similar fashion to text in Word. With an area selected, touch the editing icon on the left toolbar and touch Copy. This will store the area in the clipboard. Selecting Paste will place the contents on the clipboard in the top left of the drawing. It can then be dragged into position.

Saving the screen picture

You can capture the screen image and save it as an EPOC picture file, which can be exported to a PC or displayed in Sketch.

Save screen image as EPOC picture file	
Name	
Folder	
Disk	C
Image Type	Greyscale

Browse...   Cancel   OK
Ctrl+B

To capture the screen, press Shift+Ctrl+Fn+S. A dialog will open, into which you must enter the file name and the folder.

Loading EPOC files into Sketch

To load an EPOC file into Sketch, open the menu and select File>More>Merge in. (The keyboard shortcut is Shift+Ctrl+I.)

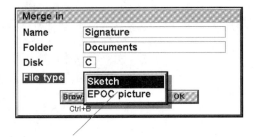

A dialog will open into which you must enter the name, folder and drive of the file you wish to load. Before touching OK, change the file type to EPOC picture.

Inserting a sketch

Agenda, Data and Word documents may contain a drawing produced with Sketch or one that has been loaded into Sketch. The second button on the right-hand toolbar in both Word and Agenda allows you to place a sketch at the current cursor position. Touch the Sketch icon and a screen similar to that of Sketch will open.

In Data, the drawing is inserted in the New Entry or Edit Entry dialog. After creating your Sketch, touch on the Done button at the top of the screen. The picture will be placed into your document. If the Sketch screen is blank when Done is touched, the Word, Data or Agenda document will not be altered. Double-touching the picture will take you back to the screen used to create the drawing, so that it may be edited. Touching the picture and then pressing Delete will remove it.

Record

Users of the Series 3a and 3c might be forgiven for skipping this chapter, in the mistaken belief that the in-built voice recorder is a variation of the program featured on the earlier computers. In fact, the voice recording facility in your Series 5 is far superior and is actually a very usable feature. The voice recording system effectively turns your Series 5 into a digital dictating machine which will enable you to record short messages which can be replayed at a later date. You can also record sounds which can be used with the alarms.

HANDY TIP

Always cover the Record and Playback buttons after use to avoid accidental use.

The main features of the recording system are a speaker (located at the back of the computer, next to the battery compartment), a microphone (on the right-hand edge of the computer, near the front) and the record/rewind/playback buttons at the front of the computer which are protected by a cover that slides back. Alongside the buttons is an LED which indicates when you are recording.

To record using the external controls on the case, slide back the cover, press and hold the Record button (left) until the red LED alongside the buttons comes on, then, whilst holding the button down, start speaking. Release the Record button when you've finished. Press Rewind (centre) followed by Play (right) to hear your recording.

You may use the voice recorder even if the computer is switched off simply by pressing the Record button. Your Series 5 will remain switched on after you have finished recording for the length of time previously determined from your entry in the System screen.

If you have password-protected your Series 5, but would like to make voice notes without having to switch on and enter the password, press and hold the Record button until it beeps. Then switch off. Although still password-protected, the machine will still respond to the external buttons to make recordings.

The recordings are tagged onto the end of the record file. As a result, the file can become quite large. Either delete the file or erase the contents when they are no longer required.

...contd

Digital sound recordings can be very large. Delete unwanted voice notes to recover the disk space.

Record

You can access the same program from the screen by touching on the Record icon from the Extras bar. The program displays a strip across the centre representing the duration of recordings in the sound file. Below are tape-recorder type buttons for Play, Forward, Rewind, Pause and Record.

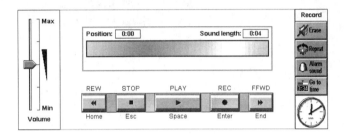

On the left is a volume control. To adjust the playback volume, touch and drag the slider up or down.

The Record program is identical to the recorder used with the external buttons, except that in the top right, Record displays the name 'Record', while 'Voice Note' appears when the external buttons are used.

The program is simple enough to operate and reflects a conventional tape recorder. Touch the Record button and speak into the microphone. Touch Rewind to move to the beginning of your recording and then Play to listen to what you have recorded. The Forward and Rewind buttons move between individual recordings in the same file.

The program is very efficient in so far as the files it creates are very compact having been compressed. But even so, 30 seconds of recording takes about 240 Kb of disk space. Clearly it will not take long before even an 8 Mb Series 5 will be full.

Creating sounds for the alarms

You can use Record to create sounds for your alarms by opening the menus and touching the Alarm sound button on the right-hand toolbar. Type in the name of the sound and press Enter. The program will store the alarm sound in a different format and place it correctly for use by either Agenda or Time. Next time you attempt to set an alarm in Agenda or in Time, you will have your new sound available with the others.

Spell

The Series 5 contains a comprehensive spelling checker which may be used alone or in conjunction with Word to check spellings. There is also a Thesaurus, which will list synonyms of words.

When the program is entered, the default state is the spelling checker. Enter a word in the space at the bottom of the screen and press Enter. The computer searches through the word list until it either finds the word, in which case it will tell you the word you entered is correct, or if it fails to recognise the word, it will list those which are close.

As soon as possible, enter all the words that are personal to you. For example, your street name, surname, children's names, car registration number, postcode, name of work place, etc.

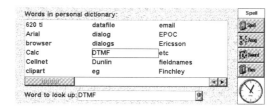

For example, if you type in the word 'sharp', the computer will tell you that the word is correct. If, however, you type 'Sharpe', the computer will tell you that that word isn't recognised and it will offer you 15 possible alternatives. It may be that 'Sharpe' is the word you require, in which case you may add it to the personal dictionary. This is best done with the keyboard shortcut Ctrl+W, although it can be found from the menu File>Personal dictionary>Add word.

The personal dictionary is case-sensitive. This means that 'Psion' and 'psion' are regarded as different words.

Any of the alternative words may be copied and then pasted into another document, usually a Word document, although it can be any program that will accept text. Double-touch the word you wish to use, press Ctrl+C to copy it, open the document and touch the place you wish the word to be pasted, then press Ctrl+V.

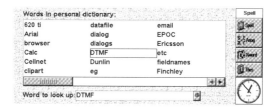

Thesaurus

The Thesaurus is used in a similar fashion to the spelling checker, except that after the word has been entered you should touch the Thesaurus icon of the toolbar on the right to display a list of synonyms.

Any of the words displayed may be copied and then pasted into another document, usually a Word document, although it doesn't have to be. Mark the word by touching it with the wand.

You may now either open the Cut, Copy and Paste menu on the left-hand toolbar and select Copy, or press Ctrl+C. Open the document into which you wish to place the word, touch the screen where you want the word to be placed and then either re-open the Cut, Copy and Paste menu and select Paste, or press Ctrl+V. The selected word will be inserted into the new document.

The other features in this program are the crossword puzzle solver and the anagram solver.

Anagram solver

If using Spell as the adjudicator for games like Scrabble, turn the 'Use personal dictionary' option off with Ctrl+U.

For fans of Channel 4's Countdown conundrum and other anagram puzzles, the anagram solver built into Spell may be of some use. Enter the letters and touch the anagram icon from the toolbar on the right to start the search.

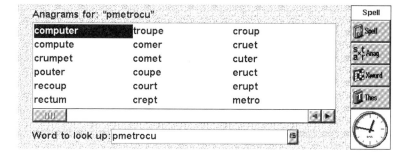

Whether or not the computer solves the conundrum within the allotted 30 seconds (or before the competitors) depends on two things. First, the word must actually be in the dictionary.

Secondly, the speed of the solution will largely depend on how near to the start of the alphabet the word actually begins with. Solutions beginning with 'A' will almost always beat the competitors, whilst you'll be lucky to win if the solution begins with 'Z'.

Crossword puzzle solver

As with the anagram solver, the answer must be in the dictionary to work, but with so many words in the dictionary, there is a strong probability that it will be.

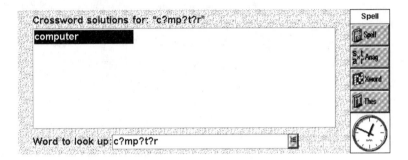

Enter as many letters from the word as you have, replacing the missing letters with a query (**?**). Touch the Xword button on the right toolbar and the computer will list all of the words that fit.

As with the other elements of this program, words may be marked, copied and then pasted into another application.

Time

There are two quite distinct parts to this program: World Time and Alarms. In order for either of these to work properly, you must first enter the correct date and time into your Series 5. If you have not already done this, go to the System screen, open the Control panel and choose Date and Time. Alternatively, from within the Time application, open the menus and select Preferences>Time and date. Initially you will enter the time in 12-hour format.

You should also set your home city. Open the menus and select Tools>Home.

Either touch the arrows on either side of the panel alongside City, or try typing in your home city.

If you wish to add a new city, it will be helpful if you know the latitude and longitude of the new city, the telephone area code and the summer time zone. Once this information has been found, you may open the menus and select Edit>Add city.

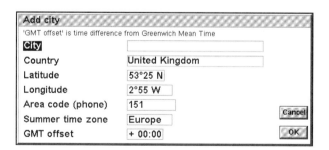

A dialog will open and the information must be entered into the appropriate places. Touch OK or press Enter when finished. You may now choose the new entry as your home city.

World Time

To access World Time, touch the Time button on the right-hand toolbar. The display shows a map of the world. On the left are two clocks. The top one should be set to your local home time: that is the city and country you previously declared as your home. Information contained in this space also includes sunrise and sunset times.

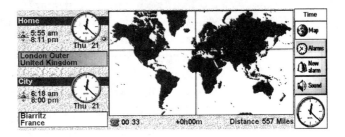

Beneath the 'home' clock is another clock, which shows the time for another named city. This too shows the sunrise and sunset times. The map will show a crosshair centred on the city. To change the city, simply touch the name once and type in the city you require. If it's not there, you will be given the nearest match (alphabetically, not geographically). Alternatively, you may double-touch the city name, in which case you'll see a dialog where the name of the city and country may be chosen. When a new city has been selected, the crosshair will now be centred on the new city, and at the bottom of the screen will be the telephone code, the time difference between there and your home city, and the distance from your home city.

You may also search for a country in the same way as for a city. If, having entered Italy, you want to know which cities in Italy have been programmed into the software, open the menus and select View>Cities in current country. Now, when entering a city, you will only get Italian ones. Don't forget to switch off this option (by going back to View>Cities in current country again). You are reminded when this option is switched on, as the word 'only' will appear alongside the country.

Alarm

The Alarm feature effectively turns your Series 5 into a very sophisticated alarm clock. You may enter up to eight alarms and select an alarm tune from the six sounds provided. Alternatively, you may record one of your own sounds using the Record feature of your Series 5 computer. See the 'Record' topic on pages 122–123 for more details.

To change to the Alarm part of the program, touch the Alarms button on the right-hand toolbar. On the right of the screen will be the usual toolbar with a clock in either analogue or digital form. On the left will be a large analogue clock, and in the centre you will see a dialog showing the eight possible alarms. Under the alarm dialog will be the time until the next alarm.

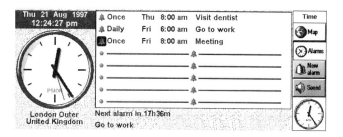

The eight alarms will initially be blank, and are represented by a bullet on the left, followed by a line with a bell at the centre. Touch the bullet corresponding to the alarm you wish to set, then touch the New Alarm button on the right-hand toolbar. Alternatively, double-touch the bullet and a dialog will open, into which you must enter the time for your alarm.

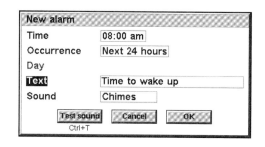

...contd

Initially you should enter the time in 12-hour clock format (e.g. five to eleven at night is 10:55), then press A for am or P for pm. (The time format can be changed by going into the System screen, opening the Control panel, selecting International and changing the format from 12-hour to 24-hour time-keeping. This will set the whole computer to run in 24-hour time mode.)

Next, you must tell the computer how often to sound the alarm by choosing the appropriate interval from the Occurrence panel.

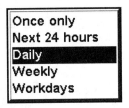

HANDY TIP

Many of these settings may be entered using the Time & Date and International sections of the Control panel in the System screen.

If you select 'Once only', you must also specify which day of the week you wish it to sound. You may define what you mean by 'Workdays' by opening the menus and selecting Tools>Workdays, then ticking all the days that constitute a workday.

You may now enter a short piece of text to remind you what the alarm is for. Finally, you must decide which of the sounds you wish to use for the alarm.

When you've entered all of the required information, touch OK or press Enter.

The alarm in use

Even if the computer is switched off, an alarm setting will cause the program to switch the computer on, sound the alarm and display the text. The only way that the alarm will not sound is if it is cancelled by you, or if the batteries are too low to actually make the sound.

The alarm will continue to sound every 15 seconds until it is silenced by pressing Enter. You may press Space to enter Snooze mode, in which case it will remain silent for five minutes before it resumes sounding the alarm every 15 seconds.

To cancel the alarm, press Esc. Once the alarm has been used, (i.e., if it was programmed to sound once, and it has sounded), it will be deleted.

Time preferences

There are several preferences which may be set in Time, many of which may also be set in the Control panel in the System screen. You should have set your home city and country from the Control panel, but if you haven't, you may do so by opening the menus in Time and going to Tools>Home.

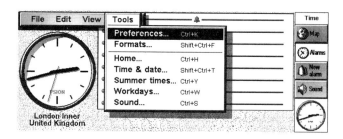

If you wish to use 24-hour format in this program only and not in any of the others, instead of selecting 24-hour time from the Control panel, open the menus, then go to Tools>Formats.

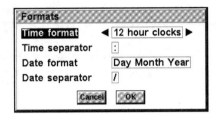

Apart from selecting 12- or 24-hour time, you may choose the time separator (initially set to a colon (:)), the date format (initially set to 'Day Month Year') and the date separator (initially a slash (/)).

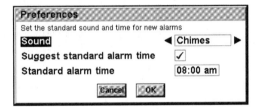

Finally, the Preferences dialog will enable you to determine the default alarm sound (i.e., the one that it uses unless you specify otherwise) and the optimum time to hear the alarm if you haven't specified another time.

Calc

If you have a Psion 5, you don't need to carry a dedicated calculator around with you too; the Psion has its own calculator application. Actually, it contains two calculators: a desktop calculator similar in function to the calculators you might find on your desk, and a fully-featured scientific calculator.

To switch between the two, touch the appropriate buttons on the right-hand toolbar.

The desktop calculator

The desktop calculator screen shows the calculator keys, with the LCD display on one side, and on the other a till roll which records your entries and the final answer. These two elements may be swapped by touching the Flip Layout button on the right-hand toolbar.

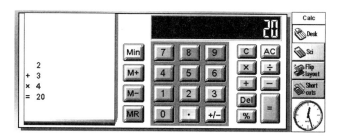

Operating the calculator is very straightforward. You may either use the keyboard keys, or touch the 'on-screen' buttons with the wand.

You may use the four arithmetic operators (+ − × ÷) to calculate between +999,999,999,999 and −999,999,999,999. Results which fall outside these limits will result in the display showing 'E'.

You may calculate percentages by using the % key.

The Delete key will delete the last character entered, providing it was a number and not a sign. E.g., 567 followed by Delete will leave 56.

Clear (C) will remove the whole of the current number, whilst All Clear (AC) will clear all numbers.

The desktop calculator also has a memory function, which uses four buttons:

Min will wipe the calculator's memory if 0 is in the display.

M+ will add the number in the calculator's display to the current contents of the memory.

M− will subtract the number in the calculator's display from the current contents of the memory.

MR (Memory Recall) which will display the contents of the calculator's memory.

Finally, the full stop is the decimal point, and the +/− key will change a positive number into a negative one and vice versa.

If you open the menus and select Tools>Shortcuts for Functions, a window will open listing all the keyboard shortcuts to the various functions. For example, Esc is the equivalent of All Clear and the letters I, O, U and Y will give the arithmetic operators without the need to use the Fn key.

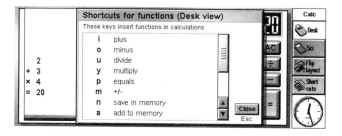

You can use the keyboard keys as well as the on-screen buttons

The answer of any calculation may be copied and pasted into another document using the Cut, Copy and Paste menu on the left-hand toolbar.

The scientific calculator

Touch the Sci button to select the scientific calculator, which includes functions for trigonometry, roots and logarithms.

The two calculators are used in a similar fashion, but the scientific calculator has 26 memories labelled A to Z. Touching the Mem button will show the contents of each memory. To enter a number into one of the memories, touch the –> button of the calculator pad and enter the name of the memory with a capital letter (as most of the lower-case letters are used for shortcuts to functions).

As with the desktop calculator, touching the Shortcuts button will display all of the keyboard shortcuts.

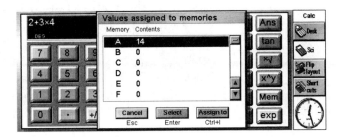

Order of precedence

An interesting feature of the two calculators is that they can apparently give different answers to the same sum. If you enter 2+3×4 into the desktop calculator, you'll get the answer of 20. This is exactly what you would expect from a standard pocket or desktop calculator. Enter the same sum into the scientific calculator and you'll get the answer 14. Again, scientific calculators would give the same result. The reason is that the desktop calculator works out the sum as you enter it: thus, 2+3 gives 5, which is then multiplied by 4 to give 20. The scientific calculator, on the other hand, looks at the whole sum in one go when you press equals (=). All arithmetic signs have a strict order (called the 'order of precedence'), which dictates that multiplication and division are calculated before addition and subtraction. Thus, the scientific calculator multiplies the 3 and the 4 together first, to give 12, to which 2 is added to give 14.

Program

The Series 5 is equipped with a powerful programming language called OPL.

Outlining the features of OPL and the principles of programming would be way beyond the scope of this book, but for those who would like to try writing some software for their Series 5, there is a manual in Word format on the PsiWin 2 CD-ROM which may be read on-screen or printed. Alternatively, Psion have produced an HTML version, which is available from their web site.

Comms

Comms is a program which provides terminal emulation and file transfer to and from other computers. It enables you to write your own instructions or scripts to carry out such tasks as automatic dialling, logging on and file transfer.

To set up the software, first touch the Setup button on the right-hand toolbar to open a dialog headed 'Communication settings'. You must select either 'Comms port' or 'Infra Red transfer'; the modem speed will be 14,400 if you're using the Travel Modem. The rest of the settings can probably be left as they are.

Further information about Comms and the script language can be obtained from Psion's web site.

Chapter Nine

Communications

In this chapter, you'll learn how to use your Series 5 to connect to the telephone and send and receive information.

Covers

Overview

The 1990's have seen a significant increase in the use of (and the need for) mobile communications. This trend appears to be increasing rapidly, with more and more people needing to contact their home or office whilst on the move.

There are numerous text or data formats which can be transmitted and received with your Series 5, providing it is connected to the correct hardware and has the correct software running.

If you need to be able to communicate whilst away from your desk, your Series 5 computer could be central to a wide range of text-based communications, including fax, email and text messaging. To enable you to send and receive text and data from your Series 5 computer, you will need to connect your computer to some other hardware.

Facsimile (fax)

The advantage of sending and receiving faxes on a computer rather than a purpose-built fax machine is that it doesn't necessarily have to be printed. Incoming faxes can, of course, be printed, in which case they will generally be of much better quality than you might expect from the average fax machine. Similarly, sending a fax is more efficient because you don't need to produce a hard copy to feed through the fax machine. You simply compose your fax on the computer and then transmit it. Outgoing faxes can be filed in the computer's memory and possibly edited or updated for later use.

EasyFax

Instead of a separate modem, you could use one of the new-generation mobile phones with a built-in modem, which require only a cable to connect the Series 5 to the phone.

EasyFax is a program for sending and receiving faxes from your Series 5 over a normal telephone line or mobile phone using the appropriate modem. It is available free from Psion's web site (the address is at the back of this book) and must first be decompressed and installed.

Setting up EasyFax

To decompress, you'll need the PC program Unzip, which is freely available from several web sites, including 3-Lib, whose address is also at the back of the book.

1 Once decompressed, the files should be copied onto a separate disk. Connect your Series 5 to the PC with the docking cable and run PsiSetup from the disk to install EasyFax onto your Series 5.

PsiWin2 should not be running when you are using PsiSetup.

2 If the installation has worked, EasyFax should be available from the Extras button on the bottom icon bar. Look at the Printer setup from either the Control panel in the System screen or from any of the applications which support printing: another printer driver will be available – Fax Print.

```
Fax Print
Epson LQ-860
Citizen PN60
General
HP DeskJet 340
HP DeskJet 660C
HP LaserJet III
HP LaserJet IV
Printer via PC
```

3 Before using EasyFax, you must first enter some settings. Start EasyFax, open the menus and select Tools>Modem settings. This leads to a dialog in which you must enter the Fax ID, which will normally be the telephone number on which you'll receive faxes. You may also enter your name in the User Name box.

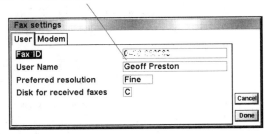

4 Next, touch the Modem tab and enter your modem details, which will probably just be the speed of your modem. The other settings are not likely to need altering.

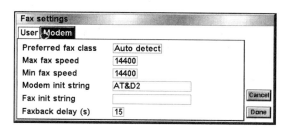

As with all data transfer of this type, it is normal practice to work 'off-line' to prepare fax files.

Sending a fax

Faxes are prepared in an application such as Word or Sketch (or any program that can print) and are then sent to EasyFax via the print dialog.

1 To do this, press Ctrl+P as you would if printing your work to a normal printer, but select the Fax Print printer driver instead of your usual printer driver.

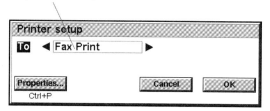

2 Touch the Properties button to open a dialog in which you may enter the file name of the outgoing fax (which will be saved in your Series 5 for future reference), the resolution (fine or medium) and whether to send now.

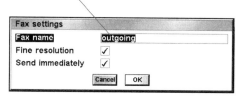

3 When the choices have been made, press Enter or touch the OK button to confirm the choices.

4 Once the settings have been made, touch the Print button and a dialog will show the fax file is being generated.

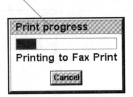

5 If EasyFax is running, you'll get an error message and the fax file will not be generated. Close down EasyFax by entering Ctrl+E from the System screen.

Whether or not you actually choose to send the fax when the fax file is generated, you may enter EasyFax, load the fax file (or double-touch the fax file to start the program) and view and send the fax.

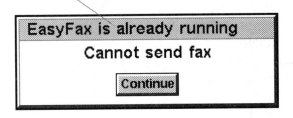

When the fax file has been created, the Series 5 will leave the current application and jump to EasyFax, where the fax file will be displayed.

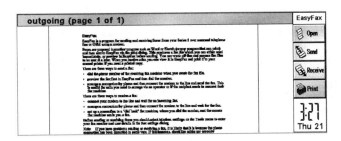

...contd

EasyFax must be closed when you do this, or you'll get a message telling you that the operation has failed.

6 If the fax file has been successfully created, a dialog will automatically be displayed. Enter the number of the recipient's fax machine and press enter to dial and send the fax. Esc will cancel the process.

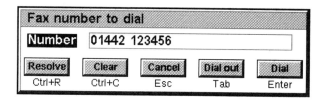

Confirmation that the fax transmission has been successful will be displayed.

You may resend the fax at any time by reloading the fax file and pressing Shift+Ctrl+S to display the Fax send dialog.

Create a fax template in Word. You could create a fancy heading using Sketch which contains all the details you need to include on every fax you send.

Receiving a fax

When you receive a fax, you can first view it in EasyFax and then, if you need a hard copy, print it.

To receive a fax, do the following:

1   Ensure that your modem is connected, then click on the Receive button on the right-hand toolbar.

2   Wait for the fax to arrive. Because this is a portable setup, it's unlikely that you'll always have your Series 5 setup for receiving faxes and so it may be necessary to contact the party from whom you wish to receive the fax to tell them when it might be convenient to transmit.

3   Once the fax has arrived, you may view it on-screen. If you wish to print it, touch the Print button on the right-hand toolbar and print in the usual way.

 Organise your faxes carefully. Use a folder for faxes to be sent, and one for received faxes.

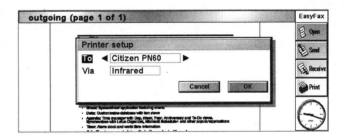

Other services requiring a modem

Apart from sending and receiving faxes, there are other services which are either available now, or which will be in due course, which will enable you to communicate with the outside world via your Series 5.

Internet access

One of the fastest-growing areas of computers is the Internet: a global network of computers which you may access from your personal computer. Software may be downloaded from the Internet – even software for your Series 5. It is now possible to access the Internet from your Series 5 computer, make the usual searches, and download text, pictures and programs just as if you were using a desktop computer. PsiInternet is available free from Psion's web site.

Electronic mail (email)

More and more people are using electronic mail. Email enables people to send text to anyone in the world, usually with a local phone call. Included in the text can also be pictures, and even computer programs, which can be compressed to speed up transmission. Even if the person to whom you're sending email is away from their desk, you can be assured that they (and only they) will read the mail. You may send the same email message instantly to a group of people, and it will arrive at the destination within minutes (or sometimes even seconds) of being sent.

Short Message Service (SMS)

The Global Standard for Mobile Communications (GSM) allows for the transmission of short text messages. Digital mobile telephone users can use this facility to send short text messages of up to 160 characters to other mobile phone users on the same network. If the recipient's phone is switched off, the message will wait in the system until the phone is switched on. Later, it will be possible to send SMS text across networks.

...contd

 HANDY TIP

Although SMS messages can only be 160 characters long, it's surprising just how much you can write in such a short space. Use it like a pager.

However, keying in messages on a telephone handset is quite tricky, as anyone who has tried it will confirm. With the correct software it is possible to enter the text on the Series 5 and then, with the correct lead to connect it to your mobile phone, transfer the message from the Series 5 into the phone before sending it.

SMS is probably the simplest communication setup currently available for your Series 5, as all that is required is a cable and a fairly simple program to run it.

There will shortly be a solution for your Series 5 which will require just a lead to connect the Series 5 to a mobile phone, in addition to the usual communications software to enable you to compose, send, receive and read messages.

SMS Fax

A little-known fact is that if you can send SMS, you can use the same equipment to send faxes. Vodaphone's Telenote Fax is a system whereby users may create a text message using their Series 5 connected to a digital phone, but before sending it, prefix the recipient's fax number with a four-digit code in order to send it as a fax. As with normal SMS messaging, it can be carried out solely on a mobile phone, but connecting the phone to the Series 5 will make the system a great deal easier to operate, as you'll be able to compose your faxes on the Series 5's keyboard rather than the 10-key pad on the phone.

In an attempt to overcome the 160-character restriction imposed by SMS, Vodaphone have thoughtfully included some short codes which are prefixed with an asterisk. When the fax is transmitted, the codes are translated into full sentences. There are currently 17 codes, which are given on the following page.

Vodaphone SMS fax codes

The 17 fax codes currently in use are as follows:

*10	CONFIRMATION
*11	URGENT
*12	FOR YOU INFORMATION
*20	I will post the requested information today.
*21	Thank you.
*22	Please call me on my mobile
*23	Please call me at the office
*24	Meeting Cancelled
*25	Please call me at home
*26	I am on my way.
*27	Have a good weekend.
*28	See you later
*29	when convenient.
*30	urgently.
*31	I look forward to speaking to you soon.
*32	Meet me at
*33	Thank you for your time at our meeting. I look forward to speaking to you again soon.

The messages translate exactly as shown, including full stops. Phrases which do not end in a full stop end with a space.

You may also send a header containing subject, recipient and sender by using a hash (#):

##Subject#Recipient#Sender#

To compose a Vodaphone Telenote Fax, type in the message as normal, using the codes as appropriate. When sending, prefix the recipient's fax number with 9741 and send as normal. Shortly you'll receive an SMS message confirming successful transmission.

The following message containing 85 characters...

##Easy Steps#Harshad#Geoff#*33 The book is now complete. *23 this afternoon or *29 *20 *31 *27 Geoff

...translates into the fax on the following page, which contains over 300 characters.

VODAFONE ♦
Telenote Fax

```
TO    :            HARSHAD
FAX NUMBER  :      
FROM  :            GEOFF
SENDER'S NUMBER  : 
SUBJECT  :         EASY STEPS
DATA  :            25/08/1997
TIME  :            12:52:28
```

Message Follows :

Thank you for your time at our meeting. I look forward to speaking
to you again soon. The book is now complete. Please call me at the
office this afternoon or when convenient. I will post the requested
information today. I look forward to speaking to you soon. Have a
good weekend. Geoff

End of Message.

VODAFONE ♦ FAX AT YOUR FINGERTIPS

The hardware

All of the communications methods discussed in this chapter require the Series 5 to be connected to the outside world via some sort of telephone. To connect any computer to a telephone line requires at least a cable with the correct plug on each end, and possibly some additional hardware, depending on exactly what you're trying to achieve. The variety of options is already bewildering and looks set to become more so, but here are the main options open to the Series 5 owner.

Modem connection

A modem (short for 'MOdulator – DEModulator') is simply an interface between a computer and a telephone line. For the Series 5 user, there are currently two main choices.

Psion Travel Modem

This is a dedicated mains- or battery-powered modem which will connect your Series 5 to a phone line via a BT-style phone socket. The Travel Modem is a 14,400 bps (bits per second) modem which will also support faxes. This hardware requires a program such as EasyFax, which is available free of charge from Psion's web site.

PC Card Modem

Among the latest technological marvels are the high-speed PC Card modems, which are about the same size as a credit card and about 5 mm thick.

Psion's PC Card modem with PCMCIA adaptor

If your Series 5 does not have a PCMCIA slot then you'll need to buy the Psion PC card adapter, which connects to the serial port at the back of the Series 5. The adapter is self-powered, which helps preserve the Series 5's batteries. Into the PC card reader (or the PCMCIA slot of your Series 5) can be inserted one of several card modems by various manufacturers.

It is beyond the scope of this book to go into all the possible variations, so I'll outline just two. The **Dacom Gold Card** by Psion is a full-featured fax modem which supports data transmission at speeds of up to 56,000 bps. This is a very versatile piece of equipment which can be used to connect the Series 5 either to land lines or to mobile phones. It is supplied with a cable to connect it to a BT phone, but if you wish to connect it to your mobile phone you'll need the correct cable and software for your particular mobile phone.

The **Nokia Cellular Data Card** will also connect into the Series 5's PCMCIA slot or PC Card reader, and offers support for Nokia GSM phones. It is supplied with a cable to connect to the mobile phone of your choice. This will work on both GSM phones (Cellnet and Vodaphone) and PCN phones (Orange and One-2-One).

HANDY TIP

Decide first on the exact nature of your requirements, then choose the mobile phone that does what you want (in other words, the phone that has the various leads and software readily available to connect to your Series 5).

Mobile phone connection

There are two conditions surrounding the connection of a Psion palmtop (or indeed any computer) to a mobile telephone. First, the telephone system must be digital and not analogue. All of the main networks either are exclusively digital, or they offer a digital service with an assortment of digital phones. Analogue phones will not work. Second, not all telephones can be connected because the necessary cables are not available. To be on the safe side, go for a high-end model from Nokia, Panasonic or Ericsson. These phones currently have the widest range of accessories, and are by far most likely to do what you want.

Mobile phones with built-in modems

At the time of writing, a couple of companies have announced that they will be manufacturing mobile phones with built-in modems which will simply connect directly to a Series 5 with the correct cable. This will eliminate the need for a Travel modem or PC Card modem for use on a GSM network. If you require connection through a land line, it is likely that you will still need a modem for the foreseeable future.

Mobile phones with built-in modems should enable you to send and receive both faxes and email, and enable you to access the Internet.

Selecting computer equipment is always going to be a bit of a lottery. Whatever you buy now, you can be sure that something better and/or cheaper is just around the corner. However, the general rule appears to be that you should not wait for something to appear that has been promised. You could find yourself waiting forever.

At present, the safest route is to select the Nokia 2110i mobile phone or one of its derivatives connected to the Vodaphone digital network. Although quite old, the 2110i does have all of the leads available.

As with all computer-related systems, technology moves very rapidly, ensuring that what is written today could be out of date tomorrow. On the horizon are total communications software packages for the Series 5, which will enable the user to access all services from one program.

Connecting a GPS receiver

In this chapter, you'll learn how to connect your Series 5 to a GPS receiver to help you find your way in your travels.

Chapter Ten

Covers

The Global Positioning System

Some years ago, the United Stated placed a constellation of satellites into orbit. They were originally for military use (in particular missile guidance), but in recent years civilians have had access to the system. At any time, at least three satellites will be 'visible' from any place on Earth, and with the correct equipment it is possible to communicate with the satellites in order to extract and compute data related to your position and speed.

 The author found the speed calculation to be about 5% high.

Reports about the accuracy of GPS vary, but with all but the cheapest GPS receivers it should be able to pin-point your position to within about 50 metres. Some receivers can get even closer. Apart from locating your position, GPS can also calculate your speed, direction and altitude. For a car driver or someone sailing a small boat, altitude is not likely to be particularly useful, but being able to compute speed means that it should also be possible to estimate the time of arrival (assuming the computer knows the destination).

Several companies manufacture and market self-contained GPS receivers which can be used in a wide variety of applications including maritime navigation, flight calculation or simply tracking your position when you're walking. GPS is a useful tool for in-car navigation, especially when abroad. In the UK, adequate road sign-posting and hand-held road maps work just as well, although they are nowhere near as much fun to use.

 If you do have GPS in the car, it should be used by someone who isn't driving.

To use your Series 5 to receive GPS signals, you need a GPS receiver, a cable to connect the receiver to the Series 5 and some software.

GPS hardware

For the Psion user, purchasing a dedicated, self-contained GPS receiver with its own input (keypad) and output (screen) is an unnecessary duplication of hardware, as the Series 5 already has a keyboard and screen. There are receivers available specifically designed to connect to a portable computer.

HANDY TIP

Keep the GPS unit away from hi-fi equipment or other electronics, as there may be interference. The GPS unit may also be less efficient if it has to look through a heated rear window or heated windscreen.

Garmin produce a range of GPS receivers, including some which are fairly low-cost but very efficient. The Garmin GPS30 is a small unit about the size of a bar of soap, and fixes onto a smooth surface with three suckers. It has no keyboard or output screen, just a cable which terminates with a 9-pin D-plug designed to connect to the serial port of a laptop PC. The unit needs a clear view of the sky, and so attaching it to the windscreen is usually suitable, although you should try to keep it away from other electrical equipment.

Connecting a GPS receiver to a Series 5

The Garmin GPS30 receiver may be connected to the Series 5 by fitting a 9-pin male D-plug to the cable from the GPS receiver, instead of the plug originally supplied. This will then connect directly into the Series 5's docking lead, which in turn plugs into the Series 5. The GPS receiver also requires power, and this is best provided by including a lead to connect it to the car's cigarette lighter socket.

BEWARE

Do not let the power line from the cigarette lighter plug touch any of the other terminals on the D-plug.

The wires from the GPS30 receiver should be connected thus:

Red	+ve	To cigarette lighter plug
Black	-ve	Pin 5 and to cigar lighter plug
Blue	data in	Pin 2
White	data out	Pin 3

All other wires are redundant for this application.

A similar, but slightly more untidy method, is to keep the existing female 9-pin D-socket on the Garmin lead and connect it to the Series 5's docking lead using a 9-pin male to 9-pin male null-modem adapter. These do exist, but you'll need to visit a specialist computer supplier to get it. Slightly easier to find is a 9-pin male to 9-pin male null modem *cable*. The trouble with this solution is that the total length of the GPS cable and the Series 5 docking cable is about 4 metres. A further 1–2 metres of null modem cable would be difficult to keep under control.

Be careful when connecting hardware to the Series 5's port. If the cable has not been correctly constructed, it could cause the program using the Series 5's port to crash, which could mean that using Ctrl+E to exit the program will not work. If this does happen, you may have to kill the program using Shift+Ctrl+Fn+K. However, this should only be used as a last resort and should be used from within the program, not from the System screen.

Psi-Mapper Gß

There are currently only two programs for the Series 5 that will support GPS, and one of those is almost free.

In terms of the number of associated data files, one of the largest programs for a palmtop computer is Steve Litchfield's geographical information system, called Psi-Mapper GB.

The complete Psi-Mapper program and its associated files take up about 400 Kb of memory and total over 350 separate files. It is unlikely that anyone will need all of them, but you'll probably need to load them all to see what is available, then discard the files you do not need.

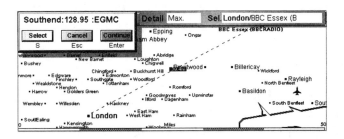

The main program draws the coastline of the UK, and additional data files (called overlays) that are supplied with the program allow the user to select which additional features are to be drawn on the map. Included with the main program are overlay files for roads, rivers, railways and town plans. There are also overlays which position all manner of miscellaneous features, including radio stations, Little Chef restaurants and places of interest.

When using PsiMapper GB to receive GPS data, the serial link must be off. From the System screen, press Ctrl+L and select Off from the dialog.

The program and all current files may be downloaded from Steve Litchfield's shareware site, 3-Lib, or by post by sending in a disk to 3-Lib. The address is at the back of the book.

When the file is unzipped, copy the contents into the System folder and run the program from the Extras bar. You will probably have enough memory in your Series 5 to keep all of the files, especially if you have the 8 Mb version. If you do need to recover some space, there will almost certainly be some Psi-Mapper files you could do without, although you'll have to delete a great number to make any real difference to the space, as the files are quite small.

There are a large number of town plans in the folder called Plans, which you'll find inside System\Apps\MapperGB.

Do not delete any file that begins with 'Map' (e.g. MapperGB, Mapicon, etc.), or the file Coastlin. Files ending with 'mp4' should not be removed, and files without a suffix (e.g. Towns) should also be kept. Many of the files are in pairs, e.g. Airfield.mbm and Airfield.mp3. If you decide that you don't need to know about airfields, delete both.

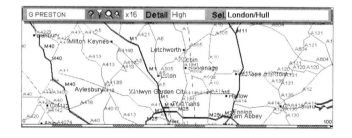

Psi-Mapper is constantly being updated and enhanced. One of the most recent additions to Psi-Mapper GB was the implementation of GPS compatibility and a moving map display, although it's only accurate to about 1 kilometre.

Once installed, open the menus and select Settings> GPS settings, or press Shift+Ctrl+G.

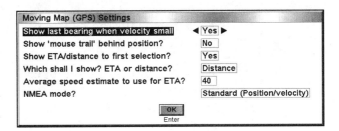

This opens a dialog in which you may select some alternatives such as deciding on whether to display the distance to your destination or the estimated time of arrival. Whichever is chosen, the output will update constantly as your journey progresses.

To use Psi-Mapper GB with a GPS receiver, open the menus and select Info>Special tools>GPS Moving Map, or simply type Ctrl+G.

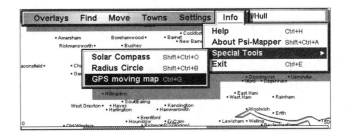

The crosshair will locate your position unless the GPS signal is weak, in which case the crosshair will be replaced with a warning symbol.

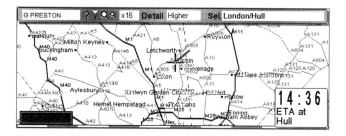

An arrow from the centre of the crosshair also indicates the direction.

Also available is Psi-Mapper London, which features over 900 locations in the London area and has several overlays including Underground stations, roads, theatres, cinemas and restaurants.

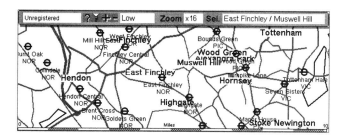

Psi-Mapper France and Psi-Mapper Ireland are also available from the 3-Lib site; these too contain all of the main features of Psi-Mapper GB and Psi-Mapper London.

En Route

If you regularly travel by car in the UK, Europe or the USA, En Route, by Palmtop BV, could prove to be an indispensable aid to planning your journeys.

En Route is a route-planning program which comes in two versions, both of which contain so much detail that they have to be supplied on CD-ROM. Both the European version and the USA version contain a staggering amount of detail, including B-roads. So great is the detail that you will only be able to install a relatively small amount of data unless you have some very large CompactFlash memory cards. En Route can interface with a GPS receiver in order to show you where on its map you are currently located.

HANDY TIP **If you require maps for several countries, place the main program and one map in the Series 5's main memory, and other maps on CompactFlash cards.**

To install En Route you'll need a PC running either Windows 3.11 or Windows 95 (or a later version), with a CD-ROM drive. PsiWin2 should not be running, and the Series 5's serial link should be switched on and running at 57,600 baud.

Place the installation CD-ROM into the drive, open it and double-click on the Install icon. Installation is then straightforward. You can choose which countries you wish to install, and the level of detail you require. You will be told how much memory you require in your Series 5.

Once the main program has been installed, you can add maps at a later date.

The display

The En Route screen normally shows the familiar toolbar on the right-hand side. This can be either moved to the left or removed altogether. Unusually, the toolbar has five buttons instead of the usual four, and the clock has been replaced with four 'sliders' which are used to adjust the on-screen detail.

The button at the very top of the screen gives the name of the program. As always, touching it will open a dialog about the currently open files.

The top button in the toolbar will switch between the map view and the table view. (The table contains textual instruction about your route.)

The button immediately under this switches between the table view and a split view, where the right half of the screen shows the map and the left part shows the table.

The exact meaning of districts may be found in the dialog which is accessed by pressing Ctrl+D.

The middle button of the group of five is labelled 'Set'. Touching this will lead to a dialog offering the choice of where to place the cursor. You may choose either the start or destination location, or any of four possible places through which the route passes.

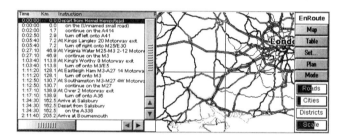

The Plan button leads to a dialog about setting a route. To plan a route you must enter a starting place and a destination. Optionally, you may also use this dialog to enter up to four intermediate places along the route.

It's worth learning some of the keyboard shortcuts to common functions and features, as it may be impractical to attempt to use the wand in the car.

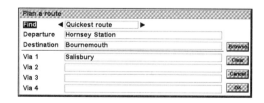

The bottom button is labelled Mode. Touching this will swap between Scroll mode and Cursor mode. When in Scroll mode, pressing the arrow keys will scroll the whole map, whilst in Cursor mode the arrow keys will move just the cursor.

...contd

En Route uses a 16-colour screen mode which requires significantly more power than 4-colour modes. If using En Route in the car, it's worth buying an adapter to plug it into the car's cigarette lighter.

In place of the clock are four 'sliders' which will vary the amount of information on the map. Touching on the left side of the sliders will reduce the detail, whilst touching the right side will increase it. The Roads slider will enable you to display all roads at their greatest detail, or just motorways when least detail is required. The Cities slider will add or remove city names in order of their size, and the Districts slider does the same for districts.

Touching the Scale slider increases or decreases the size of the map.

Many of the buttons have keyboard shortcuts...

Ctrl+Q	Choose view
Ctrl+I	Zoom in
Ctrl+O	Zoom out
Enter	Cursor/Scroll mode

En Route in use

The route instructions can be printed, which might be preferable to trying to read the Series 5 in the car.

There are several elements to this program, but the main feature is route-planning. Enter a starting point and a destination, and up to four other places via which to travel. You may either type the place names (in which case the software will offer the nearest match), or you may select the names from the menu. The program will produce a route map together with written instructions.

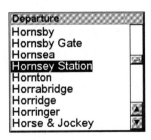

En Route preferences

Open the menus and select Map>Set Preferences, to open the tabbed dialog box you see below. Most of the options are probably set correctly for travel in the UK, though you might prefer to change from kilometres to miles.

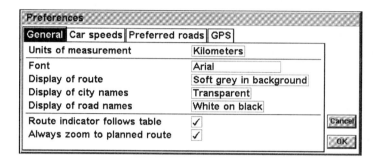

With a GPS receiver fitted, the program will place you on the map so that you can see your exact location. First switch off the serial link from the System screen, then use the GPS tab of the Preferences dialog to switch on the GPS option.

Overlays

An overlay is a file which can be placed over the map, giving additional specific information such as labels for motorway junctions.

Some overlays are included with the software and others are available from the Palmtop web site. The address is at the back of this book.

Chapter Eleven

Third-party applications

Many companies other than Psion produce software for the Series 5. This chapter introduces some of the most useful and fun applications that are available.

Covers

Overview

The Psion 3 was soon recognised as a very powerful computer, which persuaded software companies to invest a large amount of time and money in developing specialist software for it. The Series 5 is likely to receive the same support: even at the Series 5's launch, there were a dozen or more programs from third-party software houses ready to run on the new computer. The number of titles is increasing weekly.

Like the Series 3, the Series 5 is one of the few computers to be supplied with its own programming language: OPL. With only a modicum of skill, almost anyone can produce their own programs that look every bit as good as professional packages. Many amateur software authors make their work available to others as shareware software.

Shareware programs are not free. You may have obtained them freely, as indeed most are freely distributable and can be obtained by post for the cost of a stamp and a floppy disk, or downloaded from one of the numerous Psion-related web sites. You install the software on an approval basis. If after a couple of weeks you find you like the software, then you must register it. If you don't, discard it. Registering usually involves contacting the author (whose address is usually embedded into the program) and paying a small fee: usually less than £15 and frequently less than £5. In return you'll receive a registration number which, when entered into the software, registers the software as being used by you. Unregistered versions often have nag screens which constantly pop up, demanding that you register. Registration removes the nag screens and may even unlock additional features.

Ignore shareware at your own cost. Many people are put off by the fact that the programs are cheap (or free) and are written by amateurs. In fact, some shareware programs are very useful and professionally written.

Installing new programs

Currently all Series 5 software is supplied on a PC floppy disk, and due to the high cost of CompactFlash it is unlikely that this will ever change. This means that you will need a PC running Windows to install the software into the Series 5 computer.

Installation via PsiSetup

Series 5 software is frequently installed using PsiWin, but sometimes the software is supplied with an installer such as PsiSetup. This method is generally much easier to use, as the installation software determines where the various components of the program are to be located in the Series 5.

1 When using PsiSetup, you should first deactivate PsiWin. To do this, click the right mouse button on the bar alongside the clock at the bottom of the screen and select Suspend.

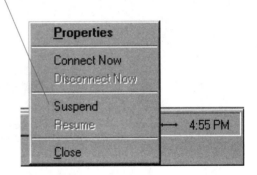

2 Place the distribution disk into Drive A: of your PC, open My Computer and choose Drive A:

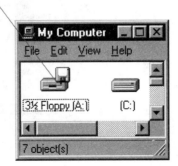

REMEMBER

The serial link must be on. To switch it on, go to the System screen and press Ctrl+L. Choose Cable and the fastest speed your PC can use.

3 When the disk window opens you should see various files, Double-click on the PsiSetup icon to run it.

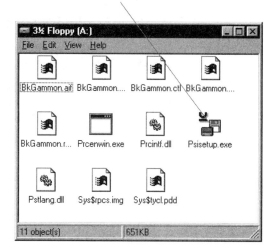

4 The title screen will appear. You should now wait while the PC tries to communicate with the Series 5.

5 Assuming the Series 5 and the PC are connected, there should be no problems. Follow the screen prompts on the PC and the software will be transferred into the Series 5. If you wish to cancel the connection, click here.

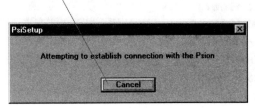

Installation via PsiWin2

Shareware software supplied on disk or downloaded from a Psion-related web site will almost always be compressed, and you'll need a program to decompress it. There are several programs which will do this for you, including some which are shareware. WinZip is one such program; it can be downloaded from:

http://www.rapidnet.com/rapidnet/tohelp/guides/ download/winzip.html

Once WinZip has been installed, load the program, click on Open and locate the zipped file. Click on the Extract button to unzip the files.

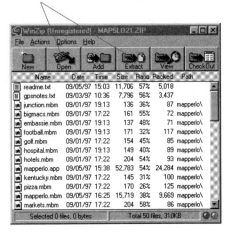

...contd

Once unzipped, installation procedure varies from program to program. In general, however, applications are installed in the Series 5 in the System\Apps folder.

The contents of this window relate to the disk in your Series 5, not your PC.

2 On your PC, move the mouse pointer to the PsiWin2 icon and double-click the left button to open a window showing the various 'disks' belonging to your Series 5. Double-click on 'Psion C' to open a window showing the contents of disk C: on the Series 5.

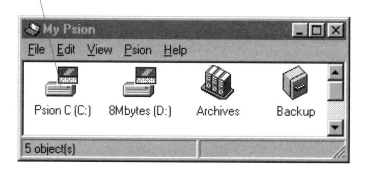

3 Double-click on the System folder.

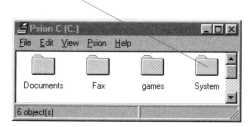

4 Now double-click on the Apps folder.

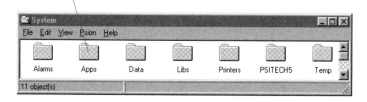

5 This should reveal all of the applications currently installed in your Series 5, including those pre-packaged with the computer. Any additional applications you wish to install should be placed in their own folder alongside the others already present.

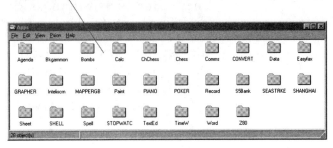

Generally, installing a program onto the Series 5 is simply a matter of dragging the files from their window on the PC into the System\Apps window belonging to the Series 5. At present, there is no unzipper for the Series 5, and so installation involves moving decompressed files into the Series 5. In due course there will be decompression programs to load into the Series 5 which will enable you to transfer the compressed file directly to the Series 5.

A text file provided with the application should give you any special information required to install it, including the name of the application folder if one has to be created.

When the application has been successfully installed, it should appear in the Extras window, which is accessed by touching the Extras button on the bottom icon bar.

Touching the application icon will start the program.

Inteliscreen

You may find that you use your Series 5 computer in particular places and at particular times, and the lighting conditions in these different situtations are likely to vary. For example, you may find that you often have to adjust the contrast and switch the backlight on and off as you try to find the best screen settings for the prevailing conditions. These conditions will most likely be the same whenever you work in any particular location location at a particular time.

Inteliscreen, by Gareth Aldread, is an application which allows the user to input times and screen setups (contrast and backlight) so that when the computer is used between the given times, the software sets up the screen perfectly.

The program is supplied as a zipped file entitled Intelisrcn.zip, and is available from the 3-Lib shareware library (the address is given at the back of this book).

Download the zip file onto your PC. Use an Unzip utility to decompress it; you'll find that you have seven files:

> add icon.mbm
> edit icon.mbm
> Inteliscrn.aif
> Inteliscrn.app
> readme.txt
> settings.dat
> time.dat

These should be placed inside a folder called Inteliscrn, within the System\Apps folder. Provided they are all present, in the correct place and correctly spelt, the working application will appear in Extras.

Access Inteliscrn by touching Extras on the toolbar at the bottom of the screen and then touching the Inteliscrn icon. The display opens with a copyright message which, when cleared, reveals the times currently programmed. These are included only as an example and can be altered to suit yourself.

Begin by entering the times of day during which you intend to use your Series 5. This may be done by either adding a new time or editing one that already exists. To edit a time, touch the Edit Time button on the right-hand toolbar. This leads to a dialog which allows you to choose which of the times you wish to edit. (Initially you may choose between 1 and 4.) Touch OK or press Enter to display a further dialog in which you enter the start and end times and which screen setting you wish to use. Note that you may not enter a start and finish time which straddles 12:00 midnight. If you wish to set such a time, you must enter two times: one leading up to midnight (e.g. 23:59:59) and then another from 00:00:00 to whichever finish time you require.

You may enter as many preset screen settings as you wish, and each must be given a name. Touch on the Add Setting button on the right-hand toolbar and a dialog will be displayed. Enter the name of the screen setting and decide whether this particular setting will have the backlight switched on. If so, touch the box alongside so that a tick appears in it. Adjust the contrast by selecting the number in the bottom box. If you want to set the contrast at that level (i.e., so that when the computer is next used it will be set at the same level) then select Set Contrast. Four settings are already provided (Day, Night, Work, Evening), and these may be edited by touching the Edit Setting button on the right-hand toolbar.

The program runs in the background, and so will not affect anything else you may be trying to do. You should only close it if you no longer want to have the display controlled for you.

Grapher

Grapher is a function graphing application which can handle eight different graphs at once. The graphs can be equalities (y=) or inequalities (y< and y>), and you may trace the graphs or find a point such as the intersection of two graphs.

The program may be download from Jamie Shotton's web site as Grapher.zip. (The address is given at the back of the book.) When this is unzipped, you should have six files:

> Grapher.aif
> Grapher.app
> Grapher.hlp
> Grapher.ini
> Icons.mbm
> ReadMe.txt

These should be placed inside a folder called Grapher, within the System\Apps folder. When installed, the program may be started from the Extras icon on the icon bar at the bottom of the screen.

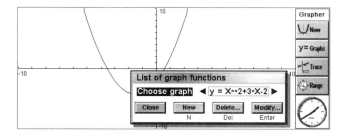

The program includes full instructions in the help file.

S5ßank

Sheet can be used very successfully to manage your financial affairs. Even easier is RMR's S5Bank, which has just been converted from the Series 3a/3c.

S5Bank can be downloaded from RMR's website as a zipped file. Once unzipped, there are 18 files to be installed in the Series 5, in the folder System\Apps\S5Bank. Three of these files are vital:

> S5Bank.aif
> S5Bank.app
> S5Bank.mbm

There are full instructions as a Word file (ReadMe) and as a text file (ReadMe.txt); a title picture (Acc_Pic), which can be optionally installed in System\Apps\S5Bank; and a file for Help (Acc_Help), which can also be installed in the same place. The remainder of the files are additional modules for such things as invoices, home accounts and fuel calculations, which may be installed if required.

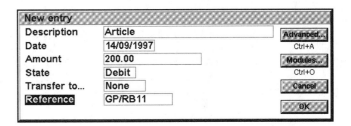

The address of RMR's web site is at the back of the book.

Games

All work and no play, it is said, makes Jack (or Jill) a dull person. Some of the professional programs and many of the shareware programs are games, so it should be useful to highlight some of the better ones available.

Chess by Purple Software

The Series 3a/3c version of Chess by Purple software was widely regarded as the best implementation of the game on a palmtop computer.

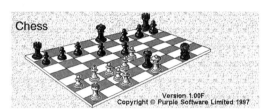

The Series 5 version takes advantage of the extra memory, better graphics and faster processor speed to produce a very playable game with many features, including a 3D board.

Apart from full instructions on how to play Chess (provided as an on-screen help file), there are several other features which will help the novice and more experienced users, such as suggested moves.

All of Purple software's programs are supplied on a PC floppy disk, and are installed using PsiSetup, which is supplied on the distribution disk.

Backgammon and Chinese Chess by Purple Software

As with Chess, this dual package was very successful on the Series 3a/c, and has been completely rewritten to take advantage of the features of the Series 5. The features are more or less the same as for Chess.

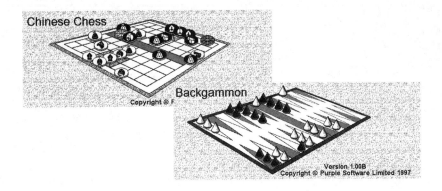

For those unfamiliar with either game, full instructions and example games are provided.

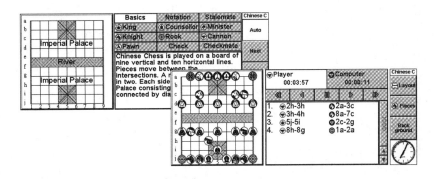

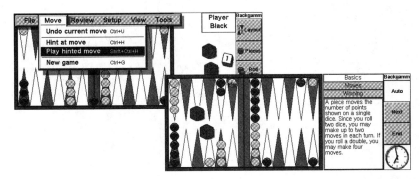

Shanghai by Ben Vaughan

The classic tile game is now available on the Series 5, and although a shareware program, is a very professional package indeed. It features over 30,000 different tile layouts, clear graphics, excellent digitised sound and full playing instructions. It is an excellent strategy game.

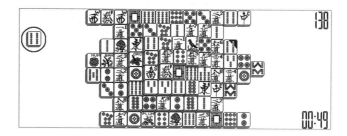

The object of the game is to match pairs of tiles. Selecting a pair removes them from the board and reveals other tiles underneath. It is most important to select the correct sequence of tiles, otherwise you won't complete the game.

SeaStrike by Mark Avey

SeaStrike is a very clever player-versus-computer implementation of the classic Battleships strategy game.

The computer places five battleships of various sizes and orientations; you do the same, and you must take it in turns to try to sink your opponent's ships. Very addictive.

Spectrum Emulator by Palmtop BV

One of the leading players responsible for the popularity of computers as a hobby was Sir Clive Sinclair. He provided the public with the first low-cost computer (the ZX80), but many people believe his finest computer was the Spectrum, a colour computer with either 16 Kb or 48 Kb of RAM, which used a television for output and a tape-recorder for the data storage. For those who still yearn to use a Spectrum, or who simply wish to take a short trip down memory lane, Palmtop BV have written a Sinclair Spectrum emulator for the Psion Series 5.

Sinclair Spectrum 48KRam Emulator

Beta Version 0.40 (Z80 emulator version 0.60)

Copyright (c) 1997 Palmtop BV The Netherlands

Supports SNA, TAP and Z80 files

Placed in the public domain by Ayal Pinkus and Pieter Geelen of Palmtop BV, june 1997.

For updates visit www.palmtop.nl

Coincidentally, some of the most popular programs for the Spectrum were written by none other than Psion.

The emulator can be downloaded from Palmtop's web site as Spectrum.zip, and when unzipped will reveal six files which should be installed in the folder System\Apps\Z80.

You can use the emulator to write programs in exactly the same way as you could on the original computer, or you can run pre-written programs.

Almost the entire catalogue of Spectrum programs is available from http://www.void.demon.nl/spectrum.html. These can be downloaded and placed into a folder called System\Apps\Z80\Games.

The emulator will support three file types: .TAP, .Z80 and .SNA files.

When the Spectrum emulator is run, you are first asked to choose the name of the file you wish to use. Since the Sinclair Spectrum used a tape-recorder to store programs, you will be told that the tape is ready.

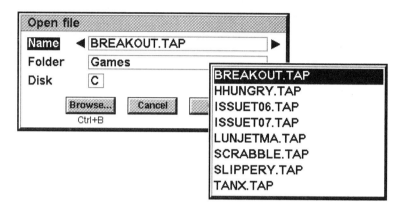

The Spectrum used a system called 'single-key entry', whereby commands as well as letters were placed on keys. The LOAD command is on the J key, and this should be followed by the name of the program you wish to load in double inverted commas (Shift+2). For example, *LOAD "beakers"* will look through the tape for a file called "beakers". *LOAD ""* on the other hand will load and run the first file on the 'tape'.

The original display was on a domestic television set, so the size of the screen on the Series 5 is quite small. On the left are details about the processor performance, and on the right a toolbar which will enable you to speed up or slow down the processor.

Some people still believe that Psion's Scrabble for the 48 K Spectrum is the best computer implementation of the classic board game.

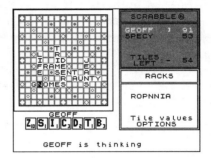

A tape-based magazine called 16/48 has also been converted to run from disk for the Spectrum emulator. Issue 7 brought back some memories.

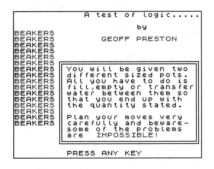

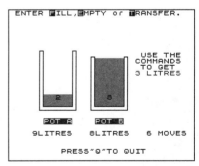

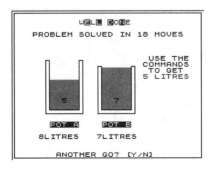

Foreign dictionaries by Palmtop ßV

To underline how versatile the Series 5 can be, Palmtop BV have released two dictionaries: French/English and German/English.

Both are installed in the same way using PsiSetup, which is supplied with the distribution disks. Each version requires about 1 Mb of memory.

Apart from translating words and phrases, the dictionaries will also solve anagrams and crosswords in the same way as Spell, but in the target language. Any text seen in the dictionaries may be copied and pasted into another document.

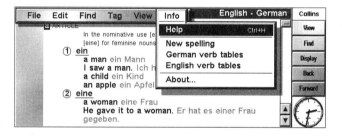

The right-hand toolbar enables you to access the most important features quickly.

View will swap between the English dictionary and the dictionary of the target language. This will happen regardless of which view you are using.

Find will open a dialogue into which you may enter a word in either English or the target language. One of the views contains links to move between the equivalent places in the two dictionaries.

Display will switch between the word list and the meanings in the currently selected language.

Back and **Forward** will move through previous searches.

Useful addresses

Chapter Twelve

This chapter lists some useful postal and email addresses which relate to the Psion Series 5. Also included are the addresses of web sites from which you can download much of the software described in the rest of this book.

Psion UK PLC 1, Red Place, London W1Y 3RE

    Phone 0990 143050 (Customer Services)

        0990 143061 (Technical Support)

    WWW http://www.psion.com

Purple Software Euston House, 81–103 Euston St,

        London NW1 2EZ

    Phone 0171 387 7777

    Email purplesoft@cix.compulink.co.uk

3-Lib Shareware 22 Grays Crescent, Woodley,

        Berks, RG5 3EN

    Email slitchfield@cix.compulink.co.uk

    WWW http://3lib.ukonline.co.uk

Clove Technology 43 Springbank Road,

        Bournemouth BH7 7EL

    Phone 01202 302796

    Email 100255.3642@compuserve.com

    WWW http://www.clove-tech.co.uk

Widget Software Ltd 121 London Road, Knebworth,

        Herts SG3 6BR

    Phone 01438 815444

Palmtop BV

Phone	+31 20 446 9469
Email	palmtop@psion.com

Ben Vaughan 25 Upper Bevendean Avenue, Brighton, Sussex BN2 4FG

Palmtop Magazine 25 Avocet Way, Bicester, Oxon OX6 0YN

Phone	01869 249 287
Email	palmtop@aol.com
WWW	http://www.palmtop.co.uk/

Garmin UK Ltd

Phone	01794 519944

Stefan Smith 16 Heath Road, Colchester Essex CO5 7HZ

Email	stef@psionworld.net

Mark Avey 17 Upper Park Street, Cheltenham, Glouc GL52 6SB

Email	mark.avey@virgin.net
WWW	http://freespace.virgin.net/ mark.avey/homepage.htm

Spectrum Software

WWW	http://www.void.demon.nl/ spectrum.html

RMR Software

	6001 Natick Ct, Burke, VA 22015 USA
Email	alanrichey@msn.com
WWW	http://members.aol.com/ alanrichey

Jamie Shotton

Email	jamies@inane.com
WWW	http://www.geocities.com/ SiliconValley/Bay/6740/

Stolen Psion Registry

	39 Union St, Cheltenham, Gloucester GL52 2JN
WWW	http://ourworld.compuserve.com/ homepages/groucho/

Maplin Electronics

Phone (Sales)	01702 554000

Index